Ho
happy
dog

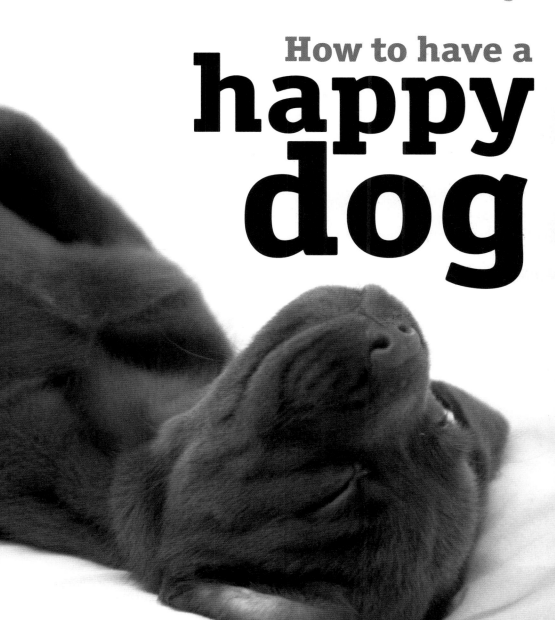

Andrea McHugh

How to have a
happy
dog

hamlyn

First published in Great Britain in 2006 by Hamlyn,
a division of Octopus Publishing Group Ltd
2–4 Heron Quays, London E14 4JP

Distributed in the United States and Canada by
Sterling Publishing Co., Inc.
387 Park Avenue South,
New York,NY 10016-8810

ISBN-13: 978-0-600-61451-7
ISBN-10: 0-600-61451-4

A CIP catalogue record for this book is available
from the British Library

Printed and bound in China

10 9 8 7 6 5 4 3 2 1

The advice given in this book should not be used as a
substitute for that of a veterinary surgeon.

No dogs or puppies were harmed in the making of this book.

In this book, unless the information is given specifically for
female dogs, dogs are referred to as 'he'. The information is
equally applicable to both male and female dogs, unless
otherwise specified.

Contents

Introduction

There is no doubt that a dog can bring pleasure into your life and make you a happier person, but do you know if your dog is as happy as he could be? You may be feeding him and walking him, but are you doing everything possible to make each day fun? Whether you already own a dog or are thinking of getting one, there are so many things you can start doing today that will ensure he really is the happiest, most contented canine in town.

Learned scholars and philosophers have been scratching their heads and trying to define happiness for centuries, but we're still no closer to explaining exactly what it is. A pleasant feeling of contentment and wellbeing seems to be the general opinion. It's certainly a state of mind that we all strive for in today's hectic modern world.

Although scientists have not yet invented a piece of equipment that can accurately measure happiness in humans or animals, they have recently confirmed that dogs laugh when they're happy. It's true! This is just one of the many fascinating facts you will discover in the pages of this book. Although we humans can't hear a dog laugh, it seems that when they do it makes other dogs a whole lot happier too. So, as you can see, it's official – happiness really is contagious!

This book will teach you how to 'read' your dog's behaviour so that he can communicate how he is feeling. You will learn what makes him tick and what ticks him off. As you read on, you will discover how to prevent problems before they begin and take advantage of all the latest scientific research to improve your dog's life. There is so much to learn, but it's so worthwhile. Knowing you have done everything possible to keep your dog brimming with joy and good health is a life-enhancing experience. Even better, it really doesn't take a great deal of time, money or effort. Happy reading ...

1 What makes dogs happy?

There is a huge difference between providing a dog with what he needs to survive, and making an effort to ensure he has a happy life. To do this, you need to know what makes a dog happy and what doesn't.

Generally speaking, dogs are real people pleasers and very much want to be involved in our lives. Ensuring that they feel secure, loved and welcome in their 'pack' is probably top of a dog's happiness wish list.

Survival basics
There are four essentials that every dog needs in order to survive:
• Food – scavenging for scraps or living off human food is unhealthy. Dogs need fresh dog food that contains all the nutrients they require.
• Water – constant access to fresh, clean drinking water is a must.
• Exercise – dogs need regular walks and activity to keep them physically healthy and mentally stimulated.
• Shelter – escape from the cold and refuge from heat are essential.

Happiness essentials
As well as the basics for survival, dogs need some extra commitments from their owners in order to be happy. These include:
• Companionship – dogs are naturally pack animals, but when they don't have access to a pack they will substitute their human/s or other family pets.
• Socializing – behaving well with other dogs and people is essential to prevent a dog becoming anxious, aggressive and isolated.
• Training – basic training will make everyone's life much easier. A well-trained dog can be taken anywhere and will be confident and happy.
• Grooming – some breeds of dog are high maintenance and require more grooming than others, but all dogs will benefit from being brushed, combed and occasionally bathed.
• Routine – dogs appreciate going out for walks and being fed at set times. This becomes even more important when they enter their senior years.
• Veterinary care – regular preventative and reactive health care will ensure that a dog has a long and healthy life.

A dog's dinner

Although your dog will readily wolf down human food, wagging his tail and looking excited when it's offered to him, such a diet will not provide all the nutrients he needs and may lead to health problems. So, what exactly should you be feeding him?

RESEARCH
Dogs require 37 essential nutrients for a complete diet. A diet lacking in just one of these nutrients is considered inadequate. Most dry foods are 'complete', as are many wet foods. However, some wet foods need dry biscuit mix added, so always check food labels carefully.

To keep your dog happy and healthy, he will need different foods during each life stage. His nutritional requirements will change as he grows from a puppy into an adult and then into a senior. Thankfully, it is easy to cater for these changing needs, as retailers stock a huge range of scientifically developed, palatable pet foods. Breed-specific food is also available. If in doubt, ask your vet for detailed advice.

Food types

Two broad types of dog foods are available:

Wet foods Conveniently packaged in cans, packs or pouches, these can contain up to 70 per cent moisture, making this a relatively expensive way to feed. Although dogs usually love these meaty foods, some owners are put off by the smell and appearance, especially in hot weather!

Dry foods Packaged in plastic cartons or bags, dry food is easy to store and has a longer shelf life than wet. Less messy to use, it generally contains less than 10 per cent moisture and is therefore more economical. On the downside, because dry food is high in calories it is easy to overfeed. Constant access to fresh, clean water is essential.

Raw deal

Because dogs are descended from wolves, many people think it is healthier and more natural to feed them a diet of raw meat. There are arguments both for and against this sort of diet, but it is worth noting that many domestic breeds of dog are unable to chew or digest raw food very efficiently – and feeding bones is always risky as splinters can pierce the intestines.

Although certain essential nutrients are lost in cooking, the cooking process will reduce the risk of bacteria being present. Because of the intensive farming methods commonly used today and the increased likelihood of contamination, it is safer to give your dog cooked meat or commercially prepared pet food.

Dogs that are fed on meat alone are likely to suffer from calcium and other deficiencies, so to keep your dog well and happy ask your vet's opinion on feeding him raw meat and the effects this may have on his health.

Foods to avoid

Chocolate Contains theobromine, which can be fatal to dogs in large quantities. It can cause vomiting, restlessness, palpitations and seizures. Pet chocolate is high in fat, so feed only as a treat.

Raisins and grapes Can be toxic to dogs and may cause renal failure.

Onions 5–10 kg (11–22 lbs) of cooked onion per kilo (pound) of bodyweight may cause anaemia.

Garlic Part of the onion family, and if eaten in large quantities may cause skin problems and asthma. If fed as a natural flea repellent, it may be advisable to feed for five days followed by a two-day break.

Lactose Found in dairy products, this is not well digested by weaned dogs.

Fruit High sugar levels and acidity may cause gastric upset.

Potatoes Cooked potatoes are not poisonous but are not easily digested. Raw green potatoes contain solanum, which is toxic to dogs.

Water

Dogs cannot store water easily and dehydration can soon be fatal. Around 60 per cent of an adult dog's body is water, and even a small loss of fluid can be serious. Dogs need about 45–50 ml of water per kilo (1 fl oz per pound) of bodyweight per day, but weather, exercise and diet also influence water intake.

> ## Happy dog tip
> Dogs can be greedy and don't always instinctively know what's good for them – so take control of your pet's diet.

Exercise and play

'Do you want to go out?' is a question your dog will be happy to hear every day! Regular exercise is vital for physical and emotional wellbeing, and a great way for you to spend time together, getting fit and having fun.

Try to incorporate some games into your daily walk to help keep your dog interested and focused on you. This is particularly useful if he's easily distracted, with a tendency to run off. Use your imagination and vary your games, but be aware of weather conditions to ensure your dog does not suffer discomfort from excessive cold or heat (see pages 14–15). Ideas for games you can enjoy playing together are given on pages 100–101.

Happy dog tip

Insufficient exercise will make your dog bored and overweight, with a tendency to destructive behaviour. Make sure you walk him every day.

'Putting him in the back yard for half an hour does not count!'

How much?

The amount of exercise your dog needs each day will change over the years, but whatever his age you should also take into account factors such as his breed, size and health (and again, be sensible about weather conditions).

Working dogs such as Border Collies and Retrievers need more exercise than toy breeds such as Yorkshire Terriers or Shih Tzus, which may be content with a walk around the block and a game of fetch in the garden. Breed societies and your vet can advise on appropriate exercise.

Puppies are still developing and their pads are soft, so aim to spend at least half your exercise time off hard ground. Avoid games that put pressure on his joints such as holding a toy in the air for him to jump up and retrieve. Don't allow him to socialize with other dogs until his vaccinations are complete.

Elderly dogs may slow down and tire more easily, but are often too excited to make this clear to their owners and will gamely go on retrieving a ball time after time, putting themselves at risk of injury. As your dog ages, be prepared to make games shorter and a little less boisterous. An older dog may become reluctant to go for a walk, particularly in winter, but wrap him up warmly and persevere, as gentle exercise will help retain fitness and mobility.

RESEARCH

A two-year study of a group of older Beagles (aged 7–11 years) concluded that regular exercise and mental stimulation plus a diet rich in antioxidants was the best way to keep dogs happy and healthy. The researchers concluded that dogs given a combination of regular exercise and the opportunity to play with other dogs and stimulating toys, were able to learn new tricks much more easily than dogs in a control group. So you can teach an old dog new tricks – provided you take care of him properly.

Playtime tips

- Exercising two or three times a day is better than one long session.
- Try to exercise your dog half an hour before feeding, and before the dog is due to be left alone. Putting him in the back yard for half an hour does not count!
- Canine treadmills are available, but do little to stimulate dogs and absolutely nothing for the human–animal bond – so get out your walking shoes, invest in some toys such as hoops and balls, and have fun together.

Indoors or out?

Your dog will not be happy if he is unable to shelter from the elements, whether rain, wind and cold or excessive heat. A dog left in a yard with no access to a cool area he can retreat to may suffer from heatstroke and dehydration, both of which can be fatal. Equally, a dog left out on a cold winter's day can suffer from exposure, particularly if he has a short or fine coat.

Even hardy working pastoral breeds such as Border Collies or German Shepherds, which many owners consider are happier outdoors, must be able to retreat to a proper outdoor kennel, shed or some other shelter that is dry, clean and draught free.

RESEARCH

Studies show that the hectic pace of modern life affects dogs as well as people. In a study of dog owners, half of those surveyed described their lives as stressful and believed this made their pets anxious. Behaviourists believe that dogs with busy working owners spend too much time alone, which can result in behaviour problems.

Puppy playpens

An indoor kennel or dog crate can help to give your pet a feeling of security, and also has the advantage of being portable so it can be taken with you if you travel to see friends. It can be particularly useful for a young puppy that needs constant supervision. A design structured from wire mesh panels will make an excellent puppy playpen that collapses down for easy storage when not in use.

Accustom your puppy to his 'den' early on, but don't leave him in there for hours on end. Your puppy (or adult dog) may be quite happy sleeping in the crate overnight, provided he has access to water and can lie on a comfortable bed, fleece or newspapers. For crate training, see pages 120–121.

The outdoor life

Some working dogs, especially those with thick coats such as the Newfoundland or Bernese Mountain Dog, are quite happy living in an outdoor kennel. Indeed, some of them will find it uncomfortable to be indoors all the time, as the temperature of a centrally heated house makes it difficult for them to settle.

If your dog lives outside, you will need to provide him with a draught-free shelter and comfortable bed, with access to shade and fresh food and water at all times. Purpose-built kennels and runs are available, designed specifically for outdoor dogs.

Hot topic

Avoid leaving your dog unattended in a car, even for short periods. Although you may have taken care to park in a sheltered spot, the sun can move around and within minutes a car can become an oven, with temperatures so high that the dog suffers heatstroke or dehydration.

Working owners

Some busy owners find it convenient to leave their dogs in an outdoor kennel and run during the day while they are at work. If you are planning to introduce this regime to your dog, do it gradually and make his kennel a fun and interesting place to be. Give him plenty of toys, hide treats for him to search for during the day, and provide a safe climbing area to encourage him to exercise.

If possible, arrange to work flexible hours so that you can return home at lunchtime to spend some quality time with your dog. And if you know you are going to be late home, make arrangements with a neighbour or friend who will be happy to attend to your dog.

'Some working dogs are quite happy living in an outdoor kennel'

Relationships

Dogs are pack animals, and in any pack there can only be one leader – a position that is often much sought after. Given the opportunity, a strong-willed dog will automatically view himself as the pack leader in your family, who is therefore entitled to the very best of everything!

Unfortunately, dogs that are allowed to become 'number one' in a household of humans make life very difficult for everyone lower down in the pack (that's you!). Many behaviour problems such as excessive barking, aggression, stealing food, hogging the sofa and so on can be very stressful, and if not dealt with early on in your relationship can be difficult to rectify without the help of a professional animal behaviourist.

For your dog, there's a fair amount of stress and responsibility involved in being the head of the household. Allowing your dog to assume this role will not make him happy, especially if he is later labelled a 'bad' dog and dumped in an animal shelter. For your dog to feel happy and relaxed at home, he must learn to accept that he is not the pack leader and never will be.

'Allowing your dog to be head of the household will not make him happy'

Did you know?

Dogs are descended from wolves and a wolf pack always has a dominant pair. However, wolves don't maintain their dominant position by fighting with pack members every day. They do it much more subtly, using body posture and attitude to make it clear who's boss.

In the dog house

Your dog must acknowledge that he is at the bottom of the family pack, with your children above him in status and you and your partner at the top. Other pets should also be taken into account: if you already have a dog and then get a new puppy, the original dog must retain his status in the household with the puppy at the bottom. This way, your existing dog will not become insecure or aggressive about a perceived threat to his position.

RESEARCH

Studies show that first-time owners are more likely to have dogs with dominance aggression, possibly due to the person's lack of experience in communicating with and handling dogs, or the breeds they choose. Dogs used for showing and breeding display less dominance aggression than average, which may be because they are trained to submit to slightly more invasive procedures.

How to be top dog

- Feed your dog after everyone else, including other pets (see page 59).
- Allocate him his own sleeping place, away from your bedroom (see page 59).
- Initiate interaction with the dog, rather than the other way round.
- Enrol in obedience classes (see Chapter 5, The Doggy Degree).
- Give attention only when he is behaving well.
- Ignore unwanted behaviour and reinforce good behaviour with praise and rewards.
- Even with puppies, be clear and consistent with house rules such as not being allowed on furniture.
- Get him neutered (see pages 60–61).
- Even though he's your best friend, never forget that he's the dog and you're head of the house. Reinforce your position as pack leader with voice tone, eye contact and using a dominant body stance.

Stimulation and training

Dogs are highly intelligent animals, which is why it is so important to try to keep them mentally stimulated. Bored, unmotivated dogs (particularly working breeds such as the Border Collie or Bearded Collie) will tend to compensate for lack of stimulation by developing their own forms of amusement – many of which are unacceptable to their owners.

An unhappy, understimulated dog may sleep excessively, chew furniture and clothing, whine and bark constantly, chase traffic or livestock, self-harm, pace up and down, exhibit aggression or become over-dependent on his owner.

Do not punish

If your dog shows destructive tendencies or other unwanted behaviour, *never* resort to physical punishment. Shouting or hitting a dog rewards attention-seeking behaviour with negative attention, and should be avoided. Try to discover the reason why he is doing something and then take steps to manage and rectify the behaviour. In addition, always check with your vet to ensure that there is no underlying physical cause for your dog's behaviour.

12 ways to a happier dog

There are many ways to keep a dog mentally stimulated that don't involve a huge time commitment: just a few minutes every day will make a huge difference to your dog's outlook on life. The key is to introduce variety and mental challenges that he will enjoy tackling. Your reward will be a dog that is happier and more alert, and a pleasure to own.

1   Consider a new activity such as agility training or heelwork to music (see Chapter 7, Exercise).
2   Try showing him in the fun classes at dog shows, such as the dog with the waggiest tail or best biscuit eater!
3   Teach him some new tricks, such as rollovers or high fives.
4   Enrol in an advanced dog training class.
5   Give your dog's toys names and teach them to him. Make a game out of asking him to fetch them for you one at a time.
6   Encourage him to think for himself with a new training method, such as clicker training (see pages 74–75).
7   Make use of interactive toys that are filled with food and dispense treats as they are moved around during play.
8   Hide treats in the house and garden and encourage your dog to find them.
9   Involve him in family life, such as taking him to the beach or on a picnic.
10 Vary the route of your walks and research new ones for you to enjoy.
11 If your dog enjoys swimming in summer, take him for walks near water or treat him to some hydrotherapy sessions.
12 Go for walks with other dog owners so that your dog has plenty of social contact.

Toy tips

- Give your dog some 'occupational therapy' with a variety of toys of different shapes, types and textures.
- Choose toys than can safely be thrown, chewed or played with, and some that can be shared with you.
- Keep one or two toys that your dog particularly enjoys as 'special treats' and use them as rewards for good behaviour.
- Avoid throwing sticks (as splinters may catch in his throat) or small stones (which he may swallow or inhale).

Happy, healthy dogs

Everyone loves to see a healthy, happy dog and it can be very distressing when a much loved pet becomes sick. Most owners would do anything to help their dog back to his nice bright eyes, cold wet nose, happy wagging tail and total enjoyment of life. Thankfully, there have been so many advances in veterinary medicine that many previously fatal diseases are now considered to be entirely preventable.

Often, the reason an owner allows their dog to become unhealthy is the misconception that preventative health care is an unnecessary expense. The logic is that if there is no obvious problem, there is no reason to visit the vet. However, taking your dog for an annual check-up, making sure his vaccinations are up to date and having him microchipped will ultimately save you a great deal of money and future heartache.

RESEARCH
A new system of genetic testing is now commercially available that allows a saliva sample to be taken and a record of the dog's genetic make-up stored, so that if he strays or is stolen his identity can be proved. It also allows for genetic testing for hereditary disease. For example, scientists hope that cataracts in Staffordshire Bull Terriers will soon be eliminated now that they are able to identify the specific gene formation that causes the problem.

Annual check-up

This is a great opportunity to discuss any concerns with your vet and receive reassurance that there are no problems with your dog. As well as giving booster vaccinations (see below), your vet will weigh and examine your dog. He will check eyes, ears, teeth, skin, coat, weight and respiration. He will also listen to your dog's heart and feel for any internal or external lumps.

Vaccinations

Vaccines are manufactured using minute, inactivated samples of a disease, which are usually injected into the dog to stimulate the immune system into producing disease-fighting antibodies (some vaccines are administered as a spray up the dog's nose). These will provide protection if the dog encounters the disease in the future.

Dogs are generally vaccinated against the following horrible diseases, some of which are highly infectious and can be fatal:

Distemper Virus that causes a runny nose, coughing, vomiting, diarrhoea and convulsions. Affected dogs become very ill and may die.

Adenoviral hepatitis Virus that attacks the liver and can cause failure.

Canine parvovirus Often fatal virus that causes severe vomiting and diarrhoea, usually in puppies.

Leptospirosis Caused by a bacterium usually carried by rats and is transmissible to humans. Dogs that go into water such as rivers are at risk. The disease causes jaundice and liver failure.

Kennel cough (infectious tracheobronchitis)
Not serious in otherwise healthy dogs, but spreads very quickly and most reputable boarding kennels will insist that dogs are vaccinated prior to boarding. Caused by a combination of three viruses (canine parainfluenza, canine adenovirus 2 and bordetella) resulting in severe coughing, which can take over a month to clear up.

Rabies Compulsory vaccination in many countries because of the risk of this fatal disease passing to humans. Not necessary for dogs in countries with rabies-free status such as the UK, Ireland, Australia, New Zealand and Japan, except for dogs that are travelling abroad (see pages 126–127).

Vaccines are effective and provide good protection. However, over recent years some people have become concerned about the necessity for and safety of vaccines. There are options to choose from regarding frequency, and if you are worried about possible adverse reactions discuss these with your vet, who will help you decide about how and when your dog should be vaccinated.

Microchipping

Getting your dog microchipped will increase his chances of being returned safely if he goes missing. It's a painless procedure that can be carried out by your vet or a trained veterinary nurse. A tiny chip, the size of a grain of rice, is injected, usually at the base of the neck. The chip is read using a scanner and details are checked against a central database.

Fleas and other parasites

Worming your dog regularly and applying flea treatments will help keep him healthy. Some dogs have severe allergic reactions to flea bites and become miserable as they constantly lick at their fur, making the area sore, inflamed and infected.

Wormers are given orally as tablets or powders that can be added to feeds, or as a paste via a syringe which you slide into your dog's mouth.

The most effective treatments to kill fleas are available from your vet, either as oral treatments, injections or capsules that are dropped onto the coat (known as spot-ons). Alternative treatments will only help to repel fleas rather than kill them.

> **Microchip tips**
> - Choose a reputable supplier (such as your vet) of high-quality microchips.
> - Keep details up to date.
> - Ask your vet to check the microchip at your dog's annual check-ups.

You wouldn't be happy if you worked for nothing and your dog is just the same, so reward him well with lavish praise, food treats, play sessions or extra attention. Every dog is different – some are motivated by food, others by play, for example – so find out what makes your dog tick. You can use your chosen reward as a way to get him to repeat a behaviour, such as coming when called or learning a new trick.

How reward works

When teaching something new, motivate your dog by rewarding him *every* time he does it right. When rewards are of high enough value (such as a favourite toy or particularly tasty food treat, see below), your dog will keep repeating the behaviour to get some more.

The key is to mark the behaviour in some way, perhaps with a verbal command, whistle or visual signal, then reward immediately. Gradually, you will be able to trigger your dog to perform a particular behaviour simply by using the command, whistle or visual signal, and maintain his motivation by rewarding sporadically. Eventually, you will be able to dispense with rewards altogether – although a little verbal praise and the odd treat is always appreciated. Using a clicker can also help to trigger behaviours (see pages 74–75).

Good dog!

You will make your dog extremely happy by rewarding him for good behaviour. This will help to keep him motivated and strengthen the bond between you. There are many types of reward you can use. Whichever you choose, don't be mean with them, particularly if you are trying to teach your dog something new, but don't overdo the calorie intake!

RESEARCH

In 1928, Russian psychologist Ivan Pavlov was studying dog behaviour and made an important discovery that he named 'classical conditioning'. When he offered food to the dogs, they began to salivate in anticipation. He then 'marked' this behaviour with a bell and soon found that the dogs would salivate involuntarily on hearing the bell, even when there was no food on offer. This forms the basis of remedial canine behaviour therapy employed today.

Types of reward

Food Choose food pieces that are small, visible, strong-smelling and unlikely to break when thrown. These can include cheese, sausage, chicken and dog biscuits. Don't use chocolate or other sugary treats that may be fattening or harmful to your dog.

Toys Keep a few favourite toys out of your dog's reach and give them to him for limited periods only, as a reward for especially good behaviour. After a few minutes, take the toy away again and keep it for next time. You may find that your dog likes toys to chew, tug or shake, or he may prefer something noisy.

Play The best kinds of play are interactive, such as throwing and retrieving a ball. Avoid play that involves teaching your dog to chase people or tug at clothes. Instead, teach him to control his instincts and stop what he's doing on command, then reward him with more play. You can combine play with a food reward if you want to.

Praise Make your dog happy with lots of verbal praise and plenty of attention. As soon as he does something right, make a huge fuss and tell him what a good dog he is, marking the behaviour with a high-toned 'Yes!'. Use a lower toned, more authoritative voice when you are discouraging unwanted behaviour.

Happy dog tip
Always have treats or a favourite toy with you. You never know when your dog will do something really well that deserves a reward.

2 Talking 'dog'

No matter how hard you try, or how intelligent he is, your dog will never fully understand the language you speak. He can, of course, learn some of your verbal commands and will constantly be trying to communicate with you in other ways. The only language he will ever speak is 'dog', which consists primarily of behaviour and body language.

The more you are able to understand what your dog is trying to tell you, the happier he will be and the better the relationship between you. Developing your ability to 'read' canine behaviour is what this chapter is all about.

Making sense of it all

Your dog will use all his senses to work out what's going on in his environment. His behaviour will be a reaction to this assessment, but remember that he is seeing things from lower down, smelling things more strongly and hearing things from much farther away than you are.

If you want to develop your understanding of what your dog is saying, you should make a point of observing him as he communicates with other dogs. You will notice that dogs 'talk' to each other using mainly body language, so the position of the tail, general posture, demeanour and expressions of the ears, eyes and mouth are crucial. Dogs try to communicate with humans in the same way, so it's important to know what that wagging tail, rollover and flattened ears really mean.

A happy dog

As a general guide, a happy, confident dog will look relaxed, hold his head up, keep his tail nice and straight and may wag it in pleasure. His ears will be pricked up and his mouth and jaw will appear relaxed. Read on to discover more about the nuances of talking 'dog'.

Mouth expressions

Your dog has a whole range of facial expressions that he uses very effectively to communicate with you and with other dogs he encounters. Regularly observing these expressions in play or, conversely, when he's feeling scared or threatened can give you a good insight into your dog's state of mind, particularly if you take into account other body language signals and the situation he is in.

By taking time to learn to pick up on your dog's expressions early enough in an interaction, you can gauge how he is feeling and become far more adept at defusing potentially difficult situations.

RESEARCH
Studies have found that the severity of a dog's bite can be gauged from his growl. American and German researchers measured growl frequency patterns for 21 breeds. The growls of larger dogs tend to show patterns that are more closely spaced, whatever the dog's head shape. It is thought that dogs may use this information to assess each other's strength.

Understanding expressions

Happy A happy, confident dog has his mouth slightly open and may be showing part of his tongue.

Worried If your dog has his mouth clenched tightly shut and is turning his head away from something he's seen, this is a signal that he is feeling insecure and worried. It is a pacifying rather than an aggressive gesture.

Curious A dog that keeps his mouth shut but is looking ahead with his ears slightly up is interested in something he has seen.

Listening Standing still with his mouth shut and ears straight up means the dog has heard something and is now trying to work out what it is.

Anxious If your dog is afraid of something he will lower his head and pull his ears back. The lips are loose or pulled back.

Threatening Your dog will curl his lips back to expose his teeth and gums. He will often do this after some other, more subtle, signals – such as looking away – have failed.

Aggressive A dog that opens his mouth, wrinkles his nose and exposes all his teeth is giving a final warning that he is about to bite.

Happy dog tip

Your dog relies on his mouth and teeth to hunt, feed, explore objects, pick them up and also to defend himself (and sometimes you!) from real or imagined threats. His muzzle, whiskers and neck are very sensitive, so always be careful when stroking him in these vulnerable areas.

Smiley dogs

Some breeds of dogs, including Dalmatians, Dobermanns and many of the terrier breeds, are actually known as 'smilers', often greeting their owners with their mouths slightly open, exposing the incisor and canine teeth. Some owners worry that this is a sign of aggression to humans because dogs never greet other dogs in this way, but in fact it is a submissive gesture.

'Some breeds of dog are actually known as smilers'

Eye contact

Imagine how unhappy your life would be if every time someone looked at you, it made you feel afraid. Happy, confident dogs need to be able to look directly at their owners and other humans without perceiving their gaze as a threatening stare. This is particularly important when dogs are in a family home, in daily contact with children who are often at eye-contact height.

As with humans, you can learn a lot from your dog's eyes and his willingness to look at you. In the wild, when one dog stares at another dog he is issuing a challenge. Some dogs are so uncomfortable making eye contact with humans that they will begin to lick their lips or pant. Sometimes, more worryingly, eye contact may trigger a sudden aggressive response.

Happy dog tip

Signs that your dog is feeling happy and relaxed are that his eyes appear soft, his ears neither up nor flat down, and when he goes into the down position, his legs are stretched out to the side.

'When a dog stares at another he is issuing a challenge'

Puppy training

Taking time to teach a puppy from an early age that eye contact can be a rewarding experience will help to increase his confidence. You can do this by spending time playing him with each day, giving him affection and food treats and at the same time encouraging him to look at you.

Threatening posture

When two dogs meet they will often stand and stare at each other until one backs down and turns his head away in a gesture of submission, shifting his weight onto his back legs. If this happens out on a walk when your dog is on the lead, you can try to defuse the situation by distracting him and turning him in the other direction.

Fear and anxiety

If you can see the whites of your dog's eyes (and can't normally) he is probably feeling very anxious and afraid of something. His eyes will be wide, his ears up and he may go into a down position with all his legs underneath him – this is so that he can launch himself from the ground at speed if he feels threatened. Dilated, enlarged pupils are a sign that a dog is feeling agitated, afraid or highly aroused.

The watch word

It can be very useful to be able to get your dog to focus his attention on you at any given time. To teach this using clicker training (see pages 74–75), every time you want the dog to look at you, give the command 'watch' and as soon as he looks at you, click and offer a food reward. With practice, he will learn to look at you on the verbal command only.

RESEARCH

Fifteen thousand years of domestication may have helped dogs to accept eye contact with humans. Hungarian researchers tested domestic dogs against hand-reared wolves, comparing their ability to find hidden food from human cues, such as following a gaze or pointing. The hand-reared wolves refused to look at humans, but the dogs were more than happy to get clues from the people by engaging in eye contact.

Tail wagging

Your dog's tail is a kind of happiness barometer that will help you to gauge his state of mind. Most people assume that when a dog is wagging his tail he's doing it simply because he's feeling incredibly happy or pleased to see them. While this is often true, it is definitely not always the case.

Tail wagging can be the equivalent of a human smile or handshake. It can also be a sign of excitement or gratitude (perhaps as you approach with his lead to take him for a walk). However, tail wagging can also be a warning, or a sign of aggression or defensiveness.

In some circumstances, perhaps when meeting a strange dog while out on a walk, tail wagging can mean your pet is insecure and worried. To read his body language effectively you will have to learn to observe his tail position, look at how he's wagging it, and also take into account the circumstances and any other signals your dog is giving out.

Talk to me

Dogs only wag their tails at things they want to communicate with and that they think will respond to them. This is how we know that tail wagging is used for social and communication purposes. A good example is the observation that your dog wags his tail when he sees you approach with a bowl of food, but won't bother wagging his tail if he simply walks into a room and finds a bowl of food on the floor.

For puppies, tail wagging can be the same as waving a white flag to call a truce if playtime gets a little rough. Puppies start wagging their tails when they are about six or seven weeks old. This is when they first start to learn social skills and enjoy play.

Friend or foe?

When meeting another dog or a human, if your dog is being friendly or curious:
- He will wag his tail from side to side in wide sweeps.
- His tail will be relaxed and drooped down naturally.
- His ears will be down.
- His fur will be smooth all along his shoulders and back.
- He will not be staring at you or another person or dog.

If your dog is giving out a warning:
- He will hold his tail out high and stiffly.
- His ears will be up.
- His eyes will be hard and staring.
- His hackles will be raised.

Tail positions

Happy and friendly Tail up, wagging confidently from side to side.
Curious Tail up, possibly slow, uncertain or irregular wagging.
Uncertain, insecure Tail low between legs, hesitant wagging.
Afraid Tail low between legs.
Aggressive Tail up or straight out from body, may be fluffed up, possibly wagging.
Predatory Tail straight, low and still (so as not to alert prey).

Marking territory

Territory marking is a fairly common problem and completely different to a lack of house training. It is often observed in multi-dog households or if a dog has not been castrated or spayed.

The behaviour known as marking is usually a dominance or anxiety issue, where a dog will lift his leg and spray a small amount of urine onto an object, place or even a person on which he wants to mark or stamp his authority. As with any other behaviour problem, the longer it is allowed to continue the more of a habit it becomes and the harder it can be to sort out.

Hormones

Uncastrated dogs will often mark their territory to attract mates and deter other male dogs. When they do this in the house, however, it can make their owners very upset, which in turn may make the dog anxious.

Territory marking often becomes a problem when a male dog reaches sexual maturity and the hormone testosterone starts to kick in, between six and nine months of age. You may notice that he starts to urinate on upright surfaces, such as lamp posts or trees when outdoors or on table legs or chairs if indoors.

Triggers

Marking is often done near the entrances to the house, on gate posts, boundary walls, door frames and so on. This is how the dog leaves his calling card, alerting other dogs to his whereabouts.

Dogs do not mark out of spite or anger, but certain events or perceived stressful situations can trigger the behaviour. Examples of these triggers include the arrival of a visitor, moving home, bringing a new baby into the house or seeing another dog walk past the window.

Castration

Early castration will usually stop marking behaviour. If you have a pedigree dog and are hesitating because you are worried that castration may not cure the problem, you can ask your vet if it is feasible to treat the dog with a chemical castration. If territory marking stops as a result of this, then you will know that permanent castration is the best option.

RESEARCH

Studies indicate that where castration is carried out, response rates (cessation of marking) vary. Of those dogs that do respond, some will do so within two weeks. The remainder will respond within six months. In a study relating specifically to urine marking in the home, castration was found to be effective in 81 per cent of cases.

Action points

- Scent marking in the home is seen more frequently in small dogs than large ones and is often related to dominance. In addition to castration, a behaviour modification programme may be required to lower the dog's status.
- A dog that has been castrated late, or only partially successfully, may continue to mark his territory. Encourage him to lift his leg in the right place with lots of verbal praise.
- Thoroughly clean any areas that your dog has sprayed using a cleaning product designed specifically to eliminate pet odours. Avoid ammonia-based products such as household bleach, as these contain some of the chemical constituents of urine and can encourage rather than deter the dog from returning to that spot. Your vet may stock products designed specifically for this purpose.

Is your dog unhappy?

Dogs use a combination of body language and behaviour to convey their physical wellbeing and emotional state of mind. When happy and healthy they are naturally inquisitive, playful and interested in their surroundings.

Unhappy dogs are none of these: they will sleep a lot, appear disinterested, may refuse to eat or be reluctant to socialize, and can also exhibit destructive or aggressive behaviours. They can also pant, whine, growl or bark excessively, and may display over-dependence on their owners.

Dog detective

Ask your vet to rule out a physical cause for depression. Once you know your dog is healthy, turn yourself into a detective. To try to find out what is making him unhappy, learn to think like a dog, and try to imagine the sights, smells and experiences he encounters in his everyday life.

Did you know?

A depressed and anxious dog may respond to a dog-appeasing pheromone (DAP) diffuser, available from veterinary surgeries. DAP is a synthetic version of a substance released by lactating bitches three to five days after they have given birth, designed specifically to calm and reassure puppies.

Common causes of unhappiness

DIAGNOSIS	COMMENTS	ACTION
Grief	Dogs may grieve following the death of an owner or a pet companion.	Stick to routines if possible; don't depend on treats and attention. In time, your dog's behaviour should return to normal.
Boredom	Very common, especially in breeds that need to be kept busy, such as terriers and collies.	Limit the time your dog spends alone. Buy toys that can be filled with treats, so he has to work to get them. Hide treats around the house, lay a garden scent trail or even build him a sand- or earth-pit to enjoy digging in. Increase his exercise and teach him new tricks to help keep him mentally stimulated.
Environment	A small toy dog or a breed that loves family life will be unhappy if made to live outside. A long-haired breed may find a heated home uncomfortable.	See Chapter 3, Choosing your happy dog, to help you decide on the right dog.
Anxiety	Can be caused by living in a multi-dog household, over-dependence on an owner or fear of loud noises.	Provide an area to which your dog can retreat and feel safe. Use of a DAP diffuser (see opposite) can be very effective.
Not being neutered	Unneutered dogs can be unhappy and frustrated, more aggressive, liable to wander off and exhibit unwanted sexual behaviours.	Have your dog neutered (see pages 60–61).

3 Choosing your happy dog

The happiest dogs are those that are able to adapt to and fit in with the lifestyle, home and time their owners are able to offer them. That's why it's essential that you choose a suitable dog right from the start – for both your sakes.

If you choose a working dog, such as a Border Collie, but are out at work all day and live in a high-rise city apartment, the dog is likely to become bored, frustrated and very unhappy, as he will not have sufficient mental or physical stimulation to satisfy his energy levels. Equally, if you are a busy individual who enjoys the outdoor life, it would be unwise to choose a high-maintenance dog, such as a Pomeranian, that will require daily grooming and less strenuous exercise. Regardless of the type of dog you choose, there are plenty of things you can do to make sure he has a stress-free, contented life.

10 ways to make your dog happy

1 Give him a routine and stick to it.
2 Make his life interesting with toys and games.
3 Keep that puppy-dog curiosity by hiding toys and treats.
4 Vary the route of his walks.
5 Try some new activities together.
6 Groom him regularly.
7 Give him jobs to do, such as find his lead or fetch his dish.
8 Provide him with his own comfortable bed.
9 Reward him when he's good.
10 Keep telling him how wonderful he is!

10 things that will make your dog unhappy

1 Harsh words.
2 Disinterest from you. Boredom.
3 Being banished away from the family.
4 Being overweight.
5 Being treated like a human baby.
6 Insufficient exercise.
7 Lack of opportunity to express himself.
8 No bed or place of his own to which he can retreat and feel secure.
9 Irregular feeding and exercise routines.
10 Ill health and lack of veterinary care.

First considerations

Getting the right dog *for you* is important in ensuring you develop a good relationship from the start and that your dog will be happy in your ownership. No matter how much you like the look or personality of a breed, don't get one unless you are certain it is going to suit your lifestyle or environment, or you will quickly have a very unhappy dog on your hands.

Also consider what you expect from your dog and what he may be able to offer you in return. Is companionship your priority, or do you want a dog that will be happy to accompany you on long walks? If walking and fitness are important to you, it may not be a good idea to choose a toy breed like a Chihuahua that could have difficulty maintaining the pace over long distances, but such a dog would make an excellent companion.

Do some research into the requirements of different breeds in terms of exercise, mental stimulation and environment to see which will match up with your priorities. If you're buying a cross-breed, try to find out as much as you can about the dog's history, how big he is likely to grow and what his life expectancy is likely to be. Only get the dog if you can provide him with everything he needs, throughout his life. Your dog's welfare and happiness depends on *you*.

What age?

Puppies need lots of attention to keep them happy. You will have to take time (perhaps off work) to help your new puppy settle in and to housetrain him. This can be hard work – although he won't stay a puppy for long!

An adult dog involves less work than a puppy, but on the downside you could inherit behaviour or health problems.

A senior dog is ideal for someone who wants a quiet companion, but old age can mean increased vet's bills and again you may inherit behaviour problems or find the dog develops them.

Can I cope?

A total mismatch of physical and emotional strengths can lead to an unhappy dog – and an unhappy owner. You will need to consider your levels of experience with pets in general and dogs in particular, your physical fitness, what living space you can provide and how houseproud you are. Only choose a breed that you are confident you will be able to manage.

Can I provide the right home?

Some smaller breeds, such as a Pug or Dachshund, are ideal for apartment living. Put a Border Collie in a city apartment, however, and you'll soon have a very frustrated, unhappy dog that will no doubt get up to all kinds of mischief to alert you to this! Other things to consider include your proximity to a main road, the attitude of your neighbours, where you can put the dog when you are at work, access to outdoors, whether your garden is dog-proof and so on.

Happy dog tip

Do your sums. As well as being able to afford enough time for the dog of your choice, you need sufficient money to pay for food, veterinary bills and other essential items (see page 51). Some dogs are more expensive to keep than others, and if you are struggling financially this may affect your relationship with your pet.

'Your dog's welfare and happiness depends on *you*'

RESEARCH

A British university found that female dogs were more easily trained in obedience and toileting, but demanded affection more than males. Males were generally found to be more active and excitable, and prone to excessive barking, owner dominance and inter-dog aggression.

Some high-maintenance breeds

Afghan Hound
Husky
Bichon Frise
French Bulldog
Border Collie
Lhasa Apso

Some low-maintenance breeds

Labrador Retriever
Golden Retriever
Border Terrier
Greyhound
Basset Hound

High or low maintenance?

A longhaired, placid dog will adore the attention of being groomed every day, and this will make him feel cared for and happy. A longhaired dog that you don't have the time or inclination to groom every day will quickly develop mats in his coat that may eventually need to be shaved off by a vet, which will definitely not make him happy!

A breed that needs lots of exercise, stimulation, time and attention several times a day will become very depressed if you can only spare the time to take him round the block morning and night. You should take all these and other 'maintenance' aspects into consideration when choosing a dog. Getting the balance right between pet and owner is the key to a long and happy relationship.

Grooming

Dogs with soft, long hair should be groomed thoroughly every day to keep their coats tangle free. This should be done methodically, starting at the head and working through to the tail, and will take at least half an hour. Dogs with short to medium-length coats should be groomed at least once a week. Bathing and coat conditioning may also be necessary, but don't overdo this as it removes the natural oils that help to keep the coat and skin healthy. Regular attention should also be given to the ears, eyes, teeth and nails (see pages 64–65).

Exercise and play

Toy breeds Lack of exercise may damage health so toy breeds should not be carried everywhere. They need at least 20 minutes of walking twice a day.

Small breeds Need at least one 30-minute walk per day, but preferably should also be taken out two more times a day – once last thing at night.

Medium-sized and larger breeds These dogs need one to two hours of exercise, spread through the day. Extra activities and games are also good.

Extra-large breeds Despite their size, most only need an hour of exercise, once or twice a day.

Maintenance requirements

A high-maintenance dog will need one or more of the following:
- Daily, thorough grooming.
- Extra professional grooming sessions.
- Hours of exercise every day.
- Extra attention due to health problems.
- Fulfilment of special physical or emotional needs, which may increase as the dog ages.
- Extra mental stimulation to keep him happy.

A low-maintenance dog will have one or more of the following:
- Placid nature.
- Low activity levels.
- Short, rough coat.
- Robust health.
- Tendency to be a (perfectly happy) couch potato unless you can persuade him otherwise!

Top 10 dogs in the USA

Labrador Retriever
Golden Retriever
German Shepherd
Beagle
Dachshund
Yorkshire Terrier
Boxer
Poodle
Chihuahua
Shih Tzu

Top 10 dogs in the UK

Labrador Retriever
German Shepherd
Cocker Spaniel
English Springer Spaniel
Staffordshire Bull Terrier
Golden Retriever
Cavalier King Charles Spaniel
West Highland Terrier
Boxer
Border Terrier

Pedigree or mongrel?

There is absolutely nothing wrong with owning a mutt or mongrel dog, and the good news is that there is no evidence that they are any more or less happy than their pedigree cousins.

Mongrels can still be beautiful to look at, and even those that are not quite so aesthetically pleasing can have fantastic personalities and make brilliant pets and loving companions. The great thing about mongrels is that they are totally unique in every way – you'll never see anyone with a dog that looks exactly like yours!

What's the difference?

Pedigree When you buy a pedigree dog you will receive papers giving full details of the dog's family tree, going back at least three generations. Pedigree dogs are sometimes called purebreds.

Cross-breed The (often accidental!) result of two different but recognized breeds mating. It may be easier to predict the characteristics of such a dog than it is for a mongrel, particularly if the breeds are from the same group, such as hunting or herding dogs.

Mongrel The result of two dogs of unknown breeding mating. This unknown lineage means it can be difficult to predict how the offspring will eventually look and behave.

Mongrels: pros and cons

In the USA, mongrels are sometimes referred to as mutts, mixed breeds, mixies or 'All Americans' – reflecting their unknown, multi-racial backgrounds! These dogs:

✔ Look unique.
✔ Often enjoy good health.
✔ Cost less to buy.
✔ Are readily available.
✔ Are cheaper to insure.
✔ Are less likely to be stolen.

✘ May look cute as puppies but not necessarily as adults.
✘ Can inherit behaviour problems.
✘ May be excluded from top showing or agility competitions.
✘ May not be fully vaccinated.

Pedigrees: pros and cons

There are over 400 pedigree breeds to choose from. With these dogs:

✔ You know exactly what the dog will look like.
✔ Health problems and behaviour traits are predictable.
✔ You will be buying a dog fully vaccinated against disease.
✔ A properly recorded family tree will be provided along with the dog.
✔ Breed clubs can provide advice and support.

✘ Your puppy will be expensive to buy.
✘ You may have to wait months for availability.
✘ Your pet may be targeted by thieves.
✘ Some are prone to health problems.

RESEARCH

Studies at the University of California, San Diego, have shown that when choosing a purebred dog people look for one that, at some level, resembles them.

When given a choice of two dogs, judges correctly matched 25 purebreds with their owners nearly two times out of three. It is thought that people choose a purebred dog which reflects their looks and temperament, while cross-breeds are chosen with a more spur-of-the-moment, instinctive feeling. Outgoing, gregarious people choose active, fun dogs while trendy, good-looking people often choose something a little unusual.

'Gregarious people choose active, fun dogs'

One dog or two?

Some people think that if they're going to have one dog they might as well have two, as the dogs will be much happier together. This is often true: dogs can really enjoy the companionship of another canine friend and watching them have fun together can be very rewarding for their owner.

However, it is a mistake to think that two dogs will be no more trouble to look after than one. You will need twice as much time for training, and it will be double the expense when it comes to food, vet's bills, insurance and boarding fees.

Caution
Inexperienced owners should avoid getting more than one dog, as it is vital they can control and train them. Otherwise, there may be great unhappiness, jealousy and distress, which in the worst cases can result in one dog fatally attacking another.

Which breeds get on best?

There is some evidence that guard dogs and some terriers are more prone to conflict in multi-dog households, while gun dogs and hounds seem to experience fewer problems.

Introducing a new dog

If you decide to get a second dog, there are a few things that will make life happier for both of them:

- Control and supervise the first few meetings.
- Don't allow your new dog or puppy constant access to your existing dog.
- Separate unsupervised dogs.
- Give the existing dog just as much time and attention as you did before.
- Male dogs may accept a new female dog more easily than another male.

More details are provided on pages 116–117.

RESEARCH

There is evidence that littermates may be harder to train, even if the owner spends the same amount of time on each dog. One reason for this is that littermates will pay attention to each other so are less likely to respond to commands. Also, one littermate is usually more assertive than the other, and the quieter one may become anxious on his own.

Adapting your routine

Here's how you can make life more harmonious for your dogs:

- Get up a little earlier each morning to give extra time and attention to both dogs.
- Try to negotiate a flexible work schedule, so that you can return home at lunchtimes to walk and spend time with the dogs.
- If you are unable to get home during the day, consider asking a neighbour or employing a pet-sitter to walk the dogs at midday.
- Working owners may be able enrol their dogs as day-boarders at a reputable establishment.
- Invest in a child stair gate or dog crate, so that you can separate the dogs when they are not supervised but they can still see each other and continue to form a bond.
- Ensure the dogs have separate places they can safely retreat to.
- Arrange separate training schedules for puppies so that they pay attention to you as the pack leader.
- Enrol them in separate puppy socialization classes so they are less distracted.
- Occasionally walk the dogs separately.
- Encourage the dogs to socialize with other dogs and behave well around human visitors.
- Keep your car clean and your dogs safe when travelling by investing in separate travel crates.

Finding your ideal dog

Use these owner profiles to help you choose your ideal dog. Read each set of questions to find which profile best describes you, then read on to see which type of dog suits you best.

Which is the right dog for you?

CITY SLICKER

Do you live in an apartment in the city?

Do you want a dog as a companion?

Do you love sitting down with your dog on your knee?

Is your favourite pastime grooming and playing with your dog?

Your ideal dog is something small, cuddly and with a low exercise requirement. A Chihuahua is ideal if you are single and want a real lap dog (but don't over-pamper). If you have children, check out the Bichon Frise – especially if you love grooming. Other dogs to look at include Dachshunds, Pomeranians and Pekingese.

FAMILY FRIEND

Do you have a large garden?

Do you want a dog to help you keep fit?

Do you want a real family pet?

Do you want a dog that is big on character, rather than size?

Your ideal dog is something in the terrier or gun dog category. Terriers are smaller, active, fun dogs but should be supervised around children. Labradors and Golden Retrievers are popular family pets, as they are generally very good with children. These dogs need regular daily walks to keep them fit and happy.

GENTLE GIANT

Do you live in the countryside in a large house?

Do you want to feel safe when you're out walking?

Do you want a dog to deter burglars?

Do you prefer big, handsome dogs rather than cute, fluffy dogs?

Your ideal dog is one of the bigger breeds such as a Great Dane. They do need a lot of exercise and training but make good family pets, although because of their size they should be supervised around children (as should other very large breeds). Other breeds that might be happy with you include the German Shepherd or, if you have a huge house and garden, one of the giant breeds such as Irish Wolfhound, Mastiff or Newfoundland.

GAME BOY

Are you a very active person?

Do you want a dog to help you meet other owners?

Are you far too busy to worry about a clean house?

Are you very competitive and do you love challenges?

Your ideal dog is a working dog such as a Border Collie, which will be very happy living with you. These dogs need to work and love challenges, so you could both enjoy agility, flyball or heelwork to music as a new hobby and a way of meeting people. Other dogs to consider include the Basset Hound or Old English Sheepdog.

4 Happy puppy, happy home

Are you ready to provide the perfect home for your new puppy? Emotions always run high when a puppy arrives, but you need to remember that he will be feeling quite stressed for some time so try to stay calm yourself. Thankfully, there are lots of things you can do to give your puppy a happy start in life – and make sure he stays happy.

This doesn't mean too much kindness and pampering through lack of exercise or an excess of treats, as this will soon make him feel decidedly unhappy. The following pages will guide you through those first crucial months, when your puppy adjusts to his new life.

Getting ready

Try to look at your home through your new puppy's eyes.

- Remember that he's small and squirmy, and can get into and under things but may not be able to escape from them later.
- Encourage family members to look after their belongings, so that anything potentially dangerous to a puppy cannot be chewed or swallowed. In particular, children's toys, games, clothing and puzzles can be very interesting to a puppy.
- Locate and pin up any electric cables out of reach of your inquisitive puppy or he may be tempted to chew them.
- This is a wonderful opportunity to train everyone in your house to get in the habit of closing toilet lids to prevent an adventurous puppy from climbing in!
- Put notices on appliances such as the dishwasher, washing machine and oven, urging everyone to check before closing the door. All of these can seem very warm, inviting places for a puppy to enjoy a quick nap.
- Pin an extra-large notice saying 'Where's the puppy?' on every door that has access to outside. Urge everyone in the house to check on the puppy's whereabouts before they go out.
- Puppy proof at least one room and use this for your puppy to enjoy the freedom to explore.

Making a new arrival happy

There are some essential items that you will need to buy for your new puppy *before* he arrives at your home. All of these are widely available from supermarkets, pet shops, or your veterinary surgeon, and your budget will dictate how much you spend and the quality of the items you buy.

Your puppy won't be any happier if his collar is studded with diamonds than if it is made of plain leather – what is important to him is that it fits properly and he can forget he's wearing it. Equally, the most expensive dog bed in the world can be made very uninviting if it is placed in a draught or next to a radiator that's too hot.

Happy dog tip
Nappy sacks and freezer bags are available in tear-off strips and are ideal to carry with you in case your puppy has an 'accident'.

Essential items

Identity disc With your name and number.

Food and water bowls Buy bowls that are large enough for your puppy to have a fresh supply available all day, and heavy enough that he can't tip them over. Bowls should be dishwasher proof or easily cleaned and non-chewable.

Dog bed An indoor crate (see entry below) may be used, or you can buy a bed. A sturdy cardboard box will do the job when your puppy is very young, but not when he is teething, as it will be easy for him to chew up so could become a choking hazard.

Bedding Buy new from a pet shop, or visit a charity shop or thrift store for a supply of blankets (also a good place to stock up on towels, for drying your dog when he comes in wet).

Poop scoop Or, alternatively, use old plastic bags.

Grooming kit You will need a comb, brush, dog shampoo, and a toothbrush and dog toothpaste.

Collar and lead These will need to be changed as your puppy gets bigger, so consider buying a cheaper set until he is fully grown.

Toys A chewy toy, a ball and toys that dispense treats when played with will all be appreciated.

Clicker To start obedience training early on.

Other useful items

Indoor kennel or crate Useful in the home and the car. If it is going to double as your dog's bed, buy one large enough to suit him when he grows.

Dog guard Keeps your dog safe and your car clean when you are travelling.

Dog coat Some breeds feel the cold more easily than others, so a dog coat will help to keep your puppy warm and happy.

Car seat covers/boot liner Muddy dogs can mess up your car, so if you don't have washable covers, spread some old blankets or towels over the seats.

'Your puppy won't be any happier if his collar is studded with diamonds'

The great outdoors

Dogs love exploring and are never happier than when they're outside, sniffing new scents and getting into mischief. For many puppies, the back yard or garden will be their first experience of the great outdoors, so make sure it is a safe place for them to be.

Use your imagination to transform your garden into a doggy paradise, full of areas to dig, hide, sunbathe, shelter and observe from. You could even plant a few tasty herbs that your puppy might enjoy nibbling!

When should he go out?

You can encourage your puppy to toilet outside as soon as possible. Train him to go in the same place by using a verbal command, such as 'toilet' and lots of praise when he responds.

Do not allow your puppy to have contact with other dogs until his vaccinations are complete at 12 weeks or so. Vaccination programmes start at eight weeks, which is often the time that a puppy moves to his new home.

Outdoor dangers

A few simple precautions will ensure your puppy stays safe outside:

Security A high boundary fence and secure gate are essential. Check these regularly to ensure there are no holes through which he can escape. Put a sign on the gate to remind visitors to close it.

Garages and sheds Keep locked so your puppy can't injure himself on tools or ingest chemicals.

Chemicals Store plant fertilizers, pesticides, paints and similar on a high shelf in your shed. Mop up spillages immediately so your puppy doesn't step in them then try to lick himself clean.

Slug pellets These often contain a chemical that is attractive to dogs but toxic. Be careful to store slug pellets in an airtight container, out of reach.

Dustbins Keep these in an area of the garden your dog cannot access, to avoid him tipping the bin over and raiding the contents.

Poisonous plants

Some of the plants in your garden may be toxic if eaten by an inquisitive puppy. These include:

- Autumn crocus *(Colchicum autumnale)*
- Angel's trumpets *(Brugmansia)*
- Bluebell *(Hyacinthoides non-scripta)*
- Burning bush *(Dictamnus)*
- Castor oil plant *(Ricinus communis)*
- Clematis
- Dumb cane *(Dieffenbachia)*
- Foxglove *(Digitalis)*
- Glory lily *(Gloriosa superba)*
- Laburnum
- Lily of the valley *(Convallaria)*
- Lupin *(Lupinus)*
- Monkshood *(Aconitum napellus)*
- Oleander *(Nerium oleander)*
- Wisteria *(Wisteria sinensis)*
- Yew *(Taxus baccata)*

The incidence of dogs being poisoned from ingesting plants is relatively low, the danger from eating slug pellets or anti-freeze significantly higher. An inquisitive puppy is probably more at risk, so supervise him when he is out in the garden and provide lots of toys to distract him from investigating plants.

Although there is no need to rush out and dig up every plant in your garden, if you are likely to worry every time your puppy approaches a shrub or flower you may feel happier getting rid of the plant. Your local garden centre or veterinary surgery will be able to offer further advice.

Caution
Avoid putting canine faeces into your compost heap as there is a risk of parasite infection. Dispose of this separately, in the household waste or a dog toilet.

Children and puppies

Your puppy is going to be an important member of your family, and as a new owner you will be keen for him to be happy and well behaved around your children. There are a few things you can do to ensure this happens, and teaching your children that the dog is not a toy and giving them some responsibility for caring for him, will really help this process.

Some breeds are more tolerant of children than others but all dogs should be supervised, particularly when they are first introduced to the younger members of the household.

RESEARCH

Studies show that children with pets tend to be more self-reliant, sociable and less selfish than those without. In a German study, 90 per cent of parents thought their dog played an educational role with their young children and improved their quality of life; 80 per cent of the children considered their dog to be their friend and confidant.

'Some breeds are more tolerant of children than others'

Happy puppy, happy child

Teach your children to respect your puppy by making his bed a 'no-go' area. This will allow him to retreat there happily and will give him a feeling of security.

Even very young children can help to care for the puppy. This will encourage them to develop a sense of responsibility and realize that the dog is a living creature, dependent on humans for survival and love. Very young children may just fetch his food bowls, find the dog biscuits or fill up his water bowl. Older children can help to groom him and take him for walks.

Explain to your children that feeding the puppy titbits from their plates will turn him into a nuisance. Keep the puppy separate in a crate or his bed at mealtimes and distract him by giving him a toy to play with.

Encourage your children to be tidy – it won't be the puppy's fault if they leave toys around and he chews them up!

First impressions

To help socialize your puppy, every time he meets new people it should be a pleasant experience. When introducing him to children, give them a toy or treat to offer him. Allow the puppy to approach the child and don't force him if he's feeling shy. Children tend to be closer to eye-contact height, so ask them not to stare at the dog but sit down and allow the puppy to take the treat. Don't let the puppy climb all over them, and tell the child to give the treat only when the puppy is nice and calm.

Happy dog tip

Bring a new puppy home midweek during term time so that he can settle in while the children are at school. When they come home, after a few minutes of play, distract them away from the puppy with a new game or video so he does not become overwhelmed.

First night nerves

The first few nights in his new home can be a little daunting for your puppy. There are so many different sights, sounds and smells for him to take in and adjust to. Be patient with him and try to prepare as much as you can beforehand, so that you are feeling happy and calm and your new puppy doesn't pick up on any stress you may have.

Decide beforehand where he's going to sleep and have everything ready for when he arrives. Your puppy will soon realize that his new home and bed are the best places in the world to be.

Happy dog tip
A few days before you pick up your puppy, leave an old T-shirt or blanket of yours with the pup's breeder to put in his litter bed. When you collect him, place this 'comfort blanket' in his travel crate and then in his bed when you reach home – the familiar scent will reassure him during the journey and on his first nights in a strange place.

New arrival

Choose a time to pick up your puppy when your diary is completely free for the next few days, so that you can devote yourself to settling him into your home. Arrive early so that you can complete all the necessary paperwork, then play with the puppy for a short time to help create a bond between you before travelling home again. Try to make everything as calm and relaxed as possible, even though you may be feeling incredibly excited and eager to get home.

On arriving home, put the puppy straight into the garden for a few minutes and give him lots of praise when he 'performs'. Play a short game with him, but ensure children know that the puppy will need lots of time to explore and sleep.

Restrict the puppy to one room for a few days, gradually extending the areas of the house he can explore. This is particularly important if you have other pets that will need to get used to the smell and sight of him. Use a stair gate to keep him in one place. (For more information on coping with other pets see pages 116–117.)

Give your puppy lots of opportunities for toilet training outside, but be prepared for some accidents as these are inevitable.

Sweet dreams

After a few active games your puppy will start to look sleepy. Put him out in the garden to relieve himself and then tuck him up in his new bed inside his crate. If he wakes in the night he may need to toilet, so try to get to him quickly without any fuss. Let him out and as soon as he's toileted settle him down again.

Avoid picking up your puppy every time he whimpers, and he should be happily sleeping through the night within about a week. You may wish to keep his crate next to your own bed for the first week or so, and then gradually move it further away so that he is sleeping contendedly in his own area within a month.

House rules

Your puppy will be much happier and more confident if you establish a routine for him early on. Knowing when he is going to be fed, when he will get a walk and when it is playtime, as well as where he is allowed to go in the house, will all help him to feel more secure.

Happy dog tip

As much as you adore your new puppy, don't allow him to rule the roost. This is your home and you should be the pack leader (see pages 16–17). What you consider cute behaviour in a puppy can become very irritating and sometimes dangerous in an adult dog.

Puppies are quite demanding of your time and attention at first, as are senior dogs, which will need more help as they grow older and less able to cope. (See Chapter 10, Happiness in old age, for more information on caring for a senior dog.)

Puppy routine

Meals Feed your puppy regularly: breakfast at 7.30 am, lunch at midday, dinner at 4pm and supper at 8pm.

Toilet training Offer your puppy toilet breaks every hour during the day, after meals and after sleeping.

Play Schedule in short play sessions throughout the day, preferably not just after he's eaten.

Training sessions Introduce your puppy to new people, noises and experiences. Using rewards, teach him his name and to come when called, as well as the 'sit' and 'down' commands (see Chapter 5, The doggy degree).

Grooming Gently brush your puppy and handle him all over, including the mouth and paws. Encourage him to accept eye contact.

Home alone

Although you want to spend every waking minute with your new puppy, you need to prepare him for those times when he will be left alone. From the beginning, leave him alone in a closed room for short periods. Start with a few minutes and then gradually build up to longer periods. Don't make a huge fuss either before you leave or when you go back into the room. Aim to make this a normal part of his day, and he will then be happy to be left alone when necessary.

Setting ground rules

Ensure that visitors and children abide by your rules for handling the puppy. Here are some you might consider:

- Never allow your puppy to bite under any circumstances, even in play. Simply say 'No' and stop playing with him immediately.
- Discourage your puppy from jumping up at people, even if they say it's not a problem.
- Give your puppy his own sleeping quarters separate from your own. Dogs that are over-dependent on their owners can become very unhappy and distressed when left alone.
- Feed your puppy after you have eaten, so that he realizes you are head of the pack in your home.
- Don't feed him titbits from the table as this encourages begging and scavenging.
- Be consistent about where you allow him to be, such as on or off the furniture. Don't allow him to sit on the sofa on the first day and then expect him to know that this area is out of bounds afterwards. A confused puppy is an unhappy one.

Neutering

Contrary to any myths you may have heard, your growing puppy will most definitely not be happier left entire. He (or she) will constantly want to roam, feel incredibly stressed, aggressive and frustrated, and be at risk of various illnesses. Furthermore, your dog won't be any happier if you allow him to breed once or her to have one litter of puppies. What your dog doesn't know, he (or she) won't miss.

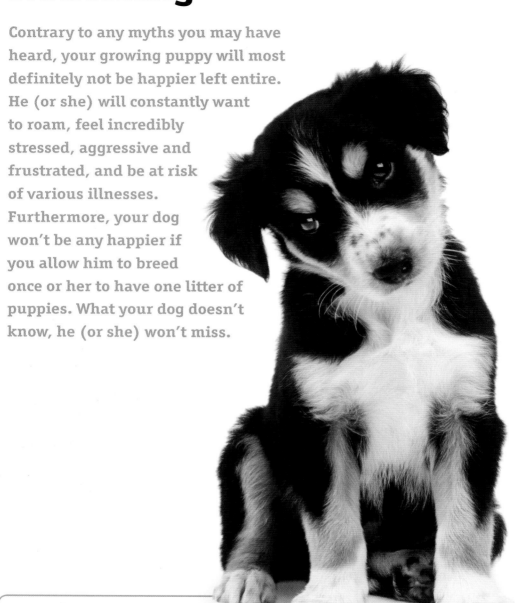

Happy dog tip
Animal shelters are full of dogs that have been picked up as uncastrated strays. Don't let this happen to your happy hound.

Straying dogs are vulnerable to infections and serious health problems, which can lead to great unhappiness for everyone concerned. Although neutering costs money, it is a long-term investment and will undoubtedly save you more on vet's bills later in your dog's life.

When should my puppy be neutered?

Male dogs become sexually mature between six and 12 months, and females between seven and 12 months. Traditionally, both female and male dogs were neutered at around six months of age but today, with safer anaesthetics and better surgical techniques, many vets advise neutering as early as eight weeks. Research has shown no adverse effects of early neutering.

Benefits of neutering

Males

- Removes the sexual urge and the chances of him wandering off (and perhaps getting hit by a car or injured in a fight).
- May reduce certain types of aggression.
- Reduces the risk of hormone-related diseases.
- Reduces the risk of anal and perineal cancers.
- Eliminates the risk of testicular cancer.
- Significantly reduces the risk of prostate gland problems.

Females

- Prevents unwanted pregnancies.
- Eliminates the mess and problems of her coming into season.
- Eliminates the urge to roam in search of a mate.
- Stops the unwanted attention of other dogs.
- Helps to prevent uterine infections.
- Helps to prevent mammary, uterine and ovarian cancer.

RESEARCH
Studies show that a dog's behavioural problems will not automatically be cured by castration alone. Some of these problems will have become habitual and self-rewarding, and further behaviour therapy will be needed. It can take several months after castration before all testosterone is removed, and you may not see a difference in behaviour for three or four months after surgery.

What neutering involves

The surgery is carried out under anaesthesia. A male dog will undergo castration, which involves the removal of both testicles. A female will have the ovaries and uterus removed. Most dogs go home quite happily the same day and suffer minimal discomfort, which is easily controlled with medication supplied by the vet.

Personality and other changes

Don't worry, your young dog should not undergo a personality change as a result of neutering. Generally speaking, behaviour will improve as he (or she) will be much calmer, more reliable and less moody. In fact, your pet will be much happier altogether, but his (or her) normal personality will still be very much in evidence.

In some breeds, neutering can change the coat texture slightly and some owners report that their dogs have a noticeable increase in appetite. If this is not addressed, you risk your pet becoming overweight. If you are worried about any health or behaviour issues that arise following neutering, ask your vet for advice.

Best behaviour

Your new puppy will probably be on his very best behaviour at first, and as a new owner you will be so anxious to make him happy that you may be accepting of more or less anything he chooses to do. However, once this initial honeymoon period is over, you may uncover a few problems. Generally speaking, these are not difficult to put right and your puppy will be happier for it.

Happy dog tip

Never lose your temper with your puppy or punish him physically. Ask your vet for advice on any behaviour you are worried about, rather than allow bad habits to become established problems that will inevitably take longer for you to remedy.

Guarding food

Although it may be cute if your puppy growls and puts his hackles up when you approach his food bowl, it definitely won't be if he's still doing this as an adult and you are too afraid to go near him. Some owners are too scared even to be in the same room as their dog while he's eating.

If your puppy exhibits this kind of behaviour, take the following steps:
- Put a small amount of food in his dish. If you use biscuits and wet food, put the biscuits in first.
- When he is eating, approach him and spoon a little wet food on top.
- Keep repeating this until the meal is finished.

Your puppy should soon get the message that you approaching the dish means more food going into it, and that you are not intending to steal his meal!

Jumping up

This often occurs because puppies are so little that people can't be bothered to bend down and greet them. Instead, they encourage the puppy to stand on his back legs and jump up towards them. It's then not fair to punish him for this as he grows bigger, but you will need to retrain him.

Ask your family and friends to ignore the puppy until he is calm and not jumping up. Train him by putting him on a lead and asking someone he knows and likes to approach you. Have a treat in your hand and when the puppy jumps up ask your helper to stand still. Put the puppy in a sit and give him the treat. Ask your assistant to approach again – only give the puppy a treat when he is sitting calmly and allowing the helper to greet him. Repeat this with everyone you meet until it becomes second nature to your pet.

Chasing and biting

Young children are naturally loud, fun and love to play – pretty much like your puppy! However, you shouldn't encourage your puppy to play chasing games with them: instead, give them some different training games to play, such as retrieving or hunting for a toy. Never allow play-biting – if this occurs, tell your child to stop the game immediately. Your puppy will soon get the message that biting ends the play session.

Barking

Barking is often triggered by the doorbell or knocker, so try to accustom your puppy to hearing this right from the start. Go outside, ring the bell and walk in, but ignore the puppy until he is quiet. Ask friends and family members to do the same. You can also ask someone with a key to ring the bell and then wait for a couple of minutes before they come in. In the meantime, give the puppy a chew or treat on his bed. This will teach him to associate the doorbell with going to his bed for a reward.

RESEARCH

According to the APBC (Association of Pet Behaviour Counsellors) in the UK, of more than a thousand dog cases that were seen, aggression towards humans accounted for 36 per cent, dog-to-dog aggression 19 per cent, and phobic and separation-related problems each 9 per cent. Male dogs were seen more often than females. The breeds most commonly seen were cross-breeds, Border Collies and German Shepherds, although this may simply be because these are among the most popular and common breeds found in the UK dog population.

Pampered pet

Your puppy should enjoy being groomed, as this is a great opportunity for the two of you to bond and spend time with each other. Some breeds need more attention than others, but all will benefit from a pampering session – which may include a massage – once or twice a week. Bathing from time to time is also beneficial.

If the weather is good, you can sit outside in the garden together and relax in the sunshine as you get to work. When you have finished the session, give your puppy a few special treats or play a game so that he remembers the entire process as a pleasant experience that he is keen to repeat.

Happy grooming

If you are grooming on a table, always cover it with a non-slip mat. Talk to your puppy all the time, praising him as he lets you groom.

1   Use a wide-toothed comb to tease out any tangles.
2   Comb out dead hairs from the undercoat.
3   Start at the head and work towards the tail with a large brush. Also brush the chest, legs and underbelly.
4   Using separate cottonwool balls dipped in a little baby oil, gently wipe clean the inside of the ears. Never poke inside the ears.
5   Use separate damp cottonwool balls to clean the eyes, starting at the inside corner and wiping outwards.
6   Check the claws, and if you are confident and have clippers, trim them. Otherwise, your vet or a professional groomer can do this for you.
7   Wipe clean the area around his bottom, trimming the hair if necessary.

Massage

Your puppy will love a five-minute massage. Rub a
small blob of light oil, such as sesame or baby oil,
into your hands and start at the head, stroking in
long sweeps down towards the tail. Pay special
attention around the cheeks, back of the neck
and the ears, which you can rub gently using your
thumb and forefinger. Gently hold and squeeze
each paw, speaking gently and calmly throughout.

If you would like to give your puppy an
aromatherapy massage, always check with your
vet that the oils you want to use are safe,
particularly if your puppy is receiving other
medication. Dogs have an incredible sense of
smell (200 million nasal receptors compared to
our 50 million), so never use undiluted essential
oils. One drop of essential oil to half a teaspoon of
carrier oil is about right. Your vet may be able to
recommend a practitioner who carries out
therapeutic aromatherapy massage.

Bathtime

In general, you should only bathe your puppy
(or dog) every two to three months, to avoid
stripping the coat of its natural oils. This will be
enough to keep him smelling sweet and his coat
in good condition.

Bathing is essential if your puppy is prone to
rolling in mud and other unsavoury things! It will
help to rid the coat of dead hair, and if he has a
skin condition your vet may prescribe a special
shampoo to help relieve the symptoms.

Bathe your puppy early in the day so that he
can dry naturally in time for bed. Groom him
thoroughly first and get everything ready that
you will need. You can use your own bath, a
shower tray or even the sink if your puppy is
small. Protect the surface of the bath with a non-
slip mat or towel that will also help to prevent
your puppy slipping.

If necessary, ask someone to help you. Using
lukewarm water, start at the head and work your
way back. Always use a dog shampoo, which is
less likely than human shampoo to irritate your
puppy or cause him to lick himself excessively
when you finish. Be especially careful around the
eyes and ears. Clean off the shampoo using a
shower hose.

Squeeze out excess water and wrap your puppy
in a towel before lifting him out of the bath and
drying him off. If a hairdryer makes him very
anxious, simply towel him off and leave him in a
warm, draught-free place to dry naturally.

5 The doggy degree

In order for your gorgeous puppy to grow into a happy, well-adjusted, sociable adult dog, he will need at least basic obedience training. It doesn't all come naturally and some dogs learn more quickly than others, but as an owner you will have to commit to whatever time and effort is required. This chapter covers the basic training every dog should undergo.

Thankfully, training can be good fun for both you and your dog, and if you enrol in classes it's also a great way to meet other owners and make new friends. Don't train your dog in long, intensive sessions – instead, make it a part of his everyday routine and he will soon understand how you want him to behave.

Benefits of training
- Your dog will be more confident.
- Your dog will respect you as leader of the pack.
- You will be relaxed taking your dog anywhere.
- Friends can enjoy visiting.
- Your dog will enjoy the extra mental and physical stimulation.
- Both of you can enjoy new activities such as agility.
- Your dog can help you by fetching the mail, his lead and so on.

Practice makes perfect
The more a dog repeats something, the more engrained that behaviour becomes. Teach your puppy to come on command by calling him to you at least 20 times a day, asking him to sit and then rewarding him with a treat or game. Do this indoors and out, and later on when he is walking off the lead. Introduce clicker training from an early age, and 'mark' behaviours you want (such as lying down on his bed) by clicking and giving a reward and a verbal command. All these aspects of training are explained in this chapter.

Happy and sociable

There's plenty you can do to help make your dog a happy and sociable pet. The early months of a puppy's life are when he is most open to learning but he can still learn when he's older, albeit at a steadier pace.

Happy dog tip

Training and socialization classes held at your veterinary clinic provide puppies and older dogs with the opportunity to meet the staff and really enjoy being there, instead of associating the sights and smells of the place with injections and other unpleasant or frightening experiences.

Dogs from rescue shelters often blossom suddenly overnight just from being placed in a loving family home. Others find everything quite stressful and need a very slow, step-by-step approach. Fears and phobias are often created by the reactions of well-meaning, anxious owners, so one of the very first things to learn is to be a relaxed, happy owner and pass your confidence on to your dog.

Early learning

If you've obtained your puppy from a reputable breeder, he will already have experienced a home environment that will have helped to socialize him. He should have been introduced to children, television, radio, vacuum cleaners, hairdryers and more. Have a chat with the breeder and check on his reactions to these things before you bring your puppy home.

The crucial socialization period for a puppy (when he is naturally at his most curious and willing to explore) ends at about 18 weeks, although this varies to some degree depending

'Fears and phobias are often created by anxious owners'

on his breed and personality. It is important to work at introducing your puppy to as many new things as possible before he reaches this age.

Back to school

Many veterinary surgeries and some dog trainers run weekly puppy socialization classes, sometimes called puppy playgroups. They are a wonderful opportunity for puppies aged between 13 and 20 weeks to learn to play happily together. Only puppies that have completed a full course of vaccinations may attend. Puppies can also learn to enjoy being handled by different people, both adults and children, in a relaxed, fun environment.

Some surgeries also run clinics for young adult dogs, in which clients can discuss general training and behaviour issues that may crop up once a dog's hormones start to kick in (see page 61).

Life experiences

You should try to introduce your puppy to as many of the following as possible:

Shops New people, sights and smells.

Lifts and elevators Enclosed spaces, strange sounds and sensations.

Street market Larger crowds, unusual smells.

Road works and construction sites Noise, smells, obstacles that block his usual route.

Different surfaces Such as laminate flooring, metal fire escape, open stairs.

Loud noises Thunder, fireworks, cars backfiring, doors slamming. CDs of loud noises are available.

Bus and railway stations Accepting a travel crate, noises, crowds.

Veterinary surgery Overcoming fear.

Variety of people Children, adults, men, women, wheelchairs; plus people wearing hats, carrying umbrellas, with facial hair, with spectacles.

Household noises Vacuum cleaner, hairdryer, doorbell, blender.

Farmyard Other animal species.

Bridges and tunnels Heights, darkness, trains and cars, water.

RESEARCH
Today, puppies selected as guide or hearing dogs are socialized in a family home during their critical first months. Studies show that the acceptance rate onto these schemes of dogs socialized in this way is far higher than before this policy was developed.

Home and dry

It's a fact of life that when you've got to go, you've got to go! And small puppies need to go quite often. Larger dogs, with bigger bladders, are generally quicker to housetrain as they can store more urine and hold onto it for longer.

Within a few days you will have a clear idea of when your puppy is most likely to need to toilet – usually this is on waking from a nap or after eating a meal, and often following a bout of playing. No matter how vigilant you are, there will inevitably be a few accidents, but stay calm and under no circumstances physically punish your puppy. He won't understand why you are angry and you will simply have a very confused and unhappy puppy on your hands.

Training strategies

Observe your puppy so that you can recognize the signs that he needs to toilet. These vary from puppy to puppy but may include sniffing, circling, whining or even jumping on your lap.

As soon as you think he needs to go, take him outside. Go out with him, even if it's cold and rainy, because otherwise he'll probably just want to come straight back inside before he has had a chance to do anything.

Take some treats with you and praise him once he has started to go, offering him a couple of treats when he has finished. You can also have a little game with him so that he associates going outside to toilet with pleasant experiences. Some owners mark the behaviour with a verbal command, such as 'toilet' or 'hurry up', especially when teaching the puppy to go in a specific place.

Avoid putting down newspapers for the puppy to toilet on in the house. He won't be able to differentiate between the newspaper you've put down for him to use and the one you haven't finished reading yet!

Dealing with accidents

If you catch your puppy mid-accident, simply call his name and open the door for him to go outside. Say the word 'out' in a high-pitched, excited tone so that he thinks outdoors is a good place to be. If you shout at him or smack him, he will simply learn to fear you and the anxiety he feels will ultimately make things worse.

Clean up any mess quickly using an odour eliminator to remove the smell and discourage the puppy from returning to that spot (see page 33). You can also use a solution of biological washing power, but test an area of your carpet before you do so. Avoid leaving an unsupervised puppy in carpeted areas.

If your puppy has been doing well for some weeks and suddenly reverts to messing in the house, you will need to find out why. Your vet can offer advice if you continue to have problems.

'No matter how vigilant you are, there will inevitably be a few accidents'

Finding a trainer

A good trainer will not teach your dog for you, but they will teach you, the owner, to train your own dog. It can be very bad for your confidence in your own ability if your dog will do anything for a trainer but chooses to ignore you!

Happy dog tip

Avoid 'quick fix' training methods, such as shock collars, at all costs. Although they may interrupt behaviour patterns, they do not get to the root cause of why a dog is behaving in a certain way.

Your dog should enjoy his training sessions and not appear apprehensive about the experience. You can help him by making training a part of his daily routine, so that it's not something he associates with a particular place or repetitive sessions and negative experiences. Remember, your dog will be happy to please you, especially if you are generous with the rewards you offer him.

Finding a trainer

If you have attended puppy socialization classes, you may already have learned the basics of training. Make enquiries about finding a reputable trainer for when your pet graduates from puppy school. Your veterinary surgery is a good place to get advice and recommendations about trainers.

Always arrange to meet the trainer and observe a few classes before committing yourself to signing up. Only use a professional trainer who advocates humane positive reinforcement methods that involve rewarding good behaviour and ignoring unwanted behaviours.

Your trainer should be someone you can communicate with easily, so ask lots of questions and look for enthusiastic answers that encourage you to ask anything without feeling silly or intimidated by your lack of knowledge.

Top 10 happy training tips

1   Wear a waist bag around the house and out on walks. Fill it with tasty treats so that you always have rewards available when your dog does something that pleases you.

2   When teaching something new, use treats or toys that he will view as high value, such as pieces of chicken or liver.

3   Use treats that are clearly visible and won't crumble when thrown down. You want the dog to focus on you rather than spend his time sniffing around for crumbs.

4   Carry a clicker in your pocket so that you can mark good behaviours throughout the day.

5   Keep some exciting toys specifically for use in training sessions.

6   If your dog becomes confused about what you want him to do, go back to an earlier stage of his training and start again.

7   Be patient with him – some dogs take longer to train than others.

8   Always end a training session on a good note, even if it means going back to something the dog can do very well such as 'sit'.

9   End the session with lots of praise, treats and a fun game or two.

10 Practise using different tones of voice. Use a lower pitched voice for low commands such as 'sit' or 'down', and a higher pitched voice for more active commands such as recall or 'fetch'.

Basic obedience training

There are a few essential commands that you should make an effort to teach your dog. Even if you teach him nothing else, he should return to you as soon as you call his name, be able to sit on command, lie down, walk to heel and be able to walk on calmly when he is off the lead.

This level of basic training will give you the confidence that you can control your dog in any situation. A happy dog loves learning something new: the mental stimulation helps to keep life interesting for him, and he too will gain confidence from his training.

'A happy dog loves learning something new'

Happy dog tip

If you have a toy breed, don't think he is too cute to bother with obedience training. Toy breeds can be highly intelligent dogs and they enjoy learning quite complicated commands and tricks.

Clicker training

Clickers are extremely useful training tools that positively reinforce and reward good behaviour. They are inexpensive and widely available from pet shops and other retail outlets.

A clicker is a plastic box with a metal tongue inside. When pressed with the thumb, this makes a distinctive double clicking sound. The clicker is small enough to hide in one hand.

The idea is that the dog soon associates the clicking sound with a reward, and once he makes this connection it is easy to get him to repeat a behaviour. The clicker can be gradually phased out once a behaviour has been learned, but is invaluable when training begins.

Introducing the clicker

Accurate timing is the key to successful clicker training. Practise until you are confident that you can use one with pinpoint accuracy. Test yourself by throwing a ball into the air and clicking before it hits the ground, or throwing it against a wall and clicking before it reaches the wall.

You will also need very tasty treats to offer the dog as soon as you have used the clicker. Begin by throwing down a treat and clicking just before the dog eats the treat and returns to you. Only click once and avoid holding the clicker close to his head or ears. Repeat this exercise several times. This will begin to create an association between the clicker and the treat.

Some people, (particularly those with less nimble fingers) prefer to keep both hands free and hide the clicker under one of their feet.

TRAINING Teaching recall

For your dog to come as soon as you call him, he needs to make the connection that returning to you is always a positive experience and worth leaving whatever interesting thing he may be doing. Here's how to teach recall:

1 When your dog is a little way away from you, call his name in an excited high-pitched voice. Call his name only once, as you want him to respond immediately. You can also get his attention by rattling a treat pot.

2 As soon as the dog turns to face you, click. When he walks towards you, reward him instantly with a treat.

3 Repeat this exercise several times, making sure you reward him generously with treats or a few seconds of play with a high-value toy each time. Once your dog returns to you quickly, you can say his name and introduce a verbal command such as 'come'. Click as he starts to walk towards you and reward him as soon as he gets back to you.

Never punish your dog for not returning to you. He will simply associate coming to you with an unpleasant experience and be even more reluctant next time. You should also avoid chasing after him, as he will think this is a great game!

Sit and stay

Teaching your dog to sit on command and stay quite happily until you tell him otherwise is very useful and forms the basis of many more advanced commands.

He should be able to sit when you ask him to, whether he is in a standing position or lying down. The 'stay' or 'wait' command can stop your dog in his tracks and can be used in many situations, such as before you put down his food bowl or to stop him jumping into the car before you've had a chance to wipe his muddy feet.

TRAINING Sitting pretty

As with many 'tricks', you can help a dog by luring his body into a position that makes it easier for him. When teaching the sit you will use a treat to lure his nose vertically upwards, which will then automatically lower his back end. You may find it easier to teach the sit with your dog on the lead.

1 Begin by holding a treat in an underhand position and call your dog to you.
2 When he is in front of you, turn your hand over so the treat is now in an overhand position.
3 Hold the treat up above the dog's nose and move your hand back slightly towards his tail. This will tip his nose up and his back end down, and he should drop into a sit.
4 Click as soon as he moves into a sit and give him the treat.
5 Repeat this several times and gradually build in the verbal command 'sit'.

RESEARCH

Scientists have proved that dogs can interpret a similar number of words to those understood by a three-year-old child.

TRAINING Wait for it!

Teaching your dog to be patient is important. Behaviourists are often asked to help dogs that have become dominant and pushy in the home, and most of these have not successfully been taught the 'stay' or 'wait' command.

1 Begin by asking your dog to come to you and sit. Instead of clicking as soon as he goes into the sit, wait for about three seconds, then click and offer a tasty reward. Repeat this several times, gradually extending the time he waits for the click to about six seconds. By doing this you will teach him that it is his patience for waiting that is being rewarded, rather than the sit. Gradually introduce the verbal command 'wait' or 'stay'.
2 Once your dog understands, take a step or two backwards. If he remains in the sit, click and return to him, giving a reward. Gradually walk further away and move slightly to each side. Click when you are at the furthest point away from the dog and then return to him, offering the reward.
3 If your dog gets up from the sit when you click but before he's had the reward, just put him back into the sit and try again.
4 Teach your dog a word that will signal to him that the wait is over, such as 'OK'.

Up and down

You may not think there is much value in teaching your dog to lie down on command, especially if it's something he does quite a lot of already! However, it's worth remembering that dogs feel quite vulnerable when they are lying down, as it is a submissive position for them to adopt.

To do this quite happily for you on command is an indication of your dog's trust and respect for you as the leader of the pack. Teaching him to lie down on command can also help to reassure visitors who come to your home, particularly if they are slightly nervous of dogs.

TRAINING Lie down

1 Begin when your dog is already standing and call him towards you. Hold a treat in the underhand position so that he can sniff it but not snatch it away from you. Gradually lower your hand, which will also lure his head and front end down.
2 Once he is in a bow position, keep your hand still and the dog's back end should drop down. As soon as he drops into the down position, click and give him the treat.
3 Repeat this several times until he drops straight into the down. Build in the verbal 'down' command and he will quickly learn to drop into position as soon as he hears the word.
4 Now try the same move, but start with the dog in a sitting position. This time lure him slightly forwards and down, so that his front legs move out a little until he can't reach any further without dropping his hindlegs down. Move the treat to the floor and as soon as he drops down, click and give him the treat.
5 Repeat this several times and build in the verbal 'down' command as you do so.

Happy dog tip

Don't confuse your dog by using verbal commands in other contexts. The 'down' command should only be used to ensure that he drops into the down position. So, if he has jumped onto a sofa or chair and you want him to get back on the floor, don't say 'down' – use another command, such as 'off'.

TRAINING On your feet

Aim to teach your dog to stand quickly and smartly on command.

1 Start with the dog in a sit. Hold a treat in the underhand position and take a step away, keeping the treat at nose level and luring your dog towards you. Be careful not to raise your hand too high or he will go back into a sit; if your hand is low he will drop into a down.
2 As soon as he stands, click and give him the treat. Repeat several times, gradually introducing the verbal 'stand' command.
3 Next teach your dog to stand from the down position. As before, hold the treat in an underhand position and step back, luring him up with your hand. His nose will come up, then his front and back legs. As soon as he stands, click and give the treat.
4 Repeat this several times and build in the verbal 'stand' command as you do so.

Caution

A thin-skinned or bony dog, such as a Greyhound or Whippet, will not be happy lying down on a cold, hard surface such as concrete. Older dogs that have lost muscle mass also find it uncomfortable.

'Teaching him to lie down on command can help to reassure visitors who come to your home'

Walking to heel

Your dog should be happy to walk at heel, both on and off the lead. However, he cannot be expected to do this if you don't take the time to teach him where the heel position is.

The heel position is next to your left leg, with your dog's nose close to your left knee. You should be able to link this command to others, such as 'sit' or 'down'. If you have more than one dog, they obviously won't both be able to walk with you in this position and it is usually the more dominant dog that will try to get there first. The other dog will then make do with walking close to your right leg. Going along with this arrangement should make it much easier to control the dogs.

Your dog should always be
focusing his gaze and his
attention towards you in
the hope that you will give
him a reward'

TRAINING Heel position

1 With your dog standing in front of you and
   slightly to your left, hold out a treat towards
   his nose.
2 Take a step back with your left leg and use the
   treat to lure the dog in an arc around you,
   until his nose is just behind your left leg. Aim
   for him to step his hindlegs to the right and as
   soon as he does, click.
3 Now bring your feet together and lure your
   dog forward in line with your knee. When
   he is standing in the correct position, give
   him the treat.
4 Stand in front of your dog and repeat the
   exercise. As he begins to understand, you
   can build in a verbal command such as
   'close' or 'heel'.
5 Practise this on both sides but mark each
   position with a different command, perhaps
   using 'close' for the left side and 'heel' for the
   right side.

As your dog becomes more proficient at getting
into position he will begin to develop 'back end
awareness'. He will soon be able to swing his
hindquarters actively around to get in close to
you as quickly as he can.

Staying focused

The more your dog focuses his attention on
you, the less likely he is to be distracted by
other dogs, sights and smells while out on a
walk. Teaching him to say close in the heel
position will help to achieve this.

TRAINING Walk on

Now that your dog understands where he should
be, you can begin to walk with him and as you
give the 'close' command he should maintain the
heel position.

1 Hold a treat in your hand, down by your side,
   and walk around the room together. Without
   stopping, occasionally give him the treat and
   immediately retrieve another one from your
   waist bag. Your dog should always be focusing
   his gaze and his attention towards you in the
   hope that you will give him a reward.
2 Eventually you can try walking in more
   complicated patterns, such as circles or
   figures-of-eight.
3 Vary your pace from fast to slow and then back
   to fast again. Gradually build up the pace until
   you can jog or skip from side to side with the
   dog remaining in position, next to your leg.

Follow the leader

It's no fun for either of you if when you are walking your dog, he pulls you about all over the place. It can also be dangerous, particularly if you are dragged towards other dogs or into the path of oncoming traffic.

Happy, relaxed dogs walk contentedly beside their owners, because they know this is the place it is most fun to be. It's also essential that you can safely control your dog as he walks next to you without a lead on, particularly if you want to try other activities such as agility.

Choosing and using equipment

Lead A short, strong lead will give you more control than a long flexi-lead. When handling a strong dog, hold the lead in both hands so you have more control if he spots something interesting and drags you in that direction.

Headcollar/harness As a last resort, there are many headcollars and harnesses on the market, designed to give owners more control. Train your dog in one of these for short sessions in the house and garden initially, and ensure that he associates the equipment with pleasant experiences. Headcollars work by exerting pressure on the back of the neck as well as the nose and it is very important not to jerk or apply continuous pressure.

TRAINING Positions please

1 Put a lead on your dog and ask him to stand in the heel position.
2 Take him for a walk, and if he starts to pull simply stop moving, plant your feet firmly and wait for him to stop or turn to face you. As soon as does, and the lead slackens off, click.
3 Walk towards him and stand with him on your left side. As soon as you are standing next to each other with a loose lead, offer him a treat.
4 Do this several times and your dog will soon begin to realize that you've got treats and will start walking closer to you in the hope of getting some more.

TRAINING Circles

Do some circle work with your dog on the lead. Keeping him on the outside of a circle will encourage him to focus on you and make it easier for him to achieve a nice flowing movement.

1 Hold the hand with the lead away from your body and walk briskly for several paces.
2 If the lead remains slack and the dog continues to focus on you, click and then stop and give him a reward.
3 Repeat in both directions.

Road sense

Encourage your dog to develop some road sense by walking him for a few minutes each day next to a busy road. You should always keep your dog on a lead near such roads, but you can accustom him to the sights and sounds and help him to realize there is nothing to fear. When crossing a road, always put your dog in a sit and wait before setting off.

Happy dog tip

Dogs that are quite bold and dominant enjoy walking on a short, tight lead. This is because they can feel you at their side as part of the pack. Nervous dogs don't enjoy being on a short, tight lead as it makes them think something scary is coming. Walking on a long, loose lead makes these dogs more confident.

6 Food and the happy dog

As you may have noticed, dogs are very motivated by food. They love it and can be extremely greedy, which means they can easily put on weight if their owners are not careful. Just as importantly, your dog must receive sufficient amounts of all the nutrients he needs to stay happy and healthy at each stage of his life.

This chapter will guide you safely through the dos and don'ts of feeding your dog, whatever his age, type or size.

Feeding for life

Lifestyle pet foods have been developed specially for puppies, adults and seniors, so check labels carefully before buying.

Your puppy will have been weaned onto solids from the age of about three weeks. When you first bring him home, continue feeding the same food as the breeder gave him. Introduce any changes very gradually after a few weeks to avoid upsetting his digestive system.

Tiny puppies need four small meals a day, reducing to three meals a day by the time they are 12 weeks old. At the age of four to five months you can split food into two meals. At about nine months your youngster should be able to cope with an adult dog diet.

Tips for a delicious dog's dinner

- Serve your dog's food in a bowl that is suitable for his size. Standing it on a non-slip mat will avoid him having to chase a sliding bowl all round your kitchen floor!
- A senior or tall dog will be extremely happy if you buy him a bowl stand to raise his food up from the floor.
- If your dog has long, floppy ears like a Spaniel or a Basset Hound, choose a deep, narrow bowl to help prevent his ears drooping into the food.
- Check labels to ensure you are feeding the correct amount.
- Remove food from the refrigerator an hour before feeding so that it can warm to room temperature, which will make it more palatable.
- Dispose of uneaten wet food immediately, as it will quickly become stale and contaminated by flies.
- Wash food bowls immediately. Bacteria multiply quickly in dirty bowls and can cause a nasty gastric upset.
- Ensure that he always has a fresh supply of water.

Food, glorious food!

One of the best ways you can make your dog happy is to feed him the best food you can afford. Feeding commercially prepared pet food is probably the most convenient method for busy owners, unless you happen to be extremely knowledgeable about canine nutrition and have many spare hours to prepare food from raw ingredients.

Commercial pet food contains enough meat, fish and cereals, vitamins and minerals to satisfy your adult dog's nutritional needs in one or two daily feeds, so is the best choice for most owners.

Food and behaviour

'We are what we eat' and our dogs are no different. Some behaviour problems can be attributed to a change in diet and individual dogs may react to different levels of sugar, chemicals and preservatives in their food. Certain colourants have been linked to behavioural problems, and there is some anecdotal evidence that indicates that maize can trigger hyperactivity and other problems in some dogs.

If your dog exhibits changes in behaviour or mood and there is no obvious physical reason for this, it may be worth looking at his diet to see if you have recently introduced any changes to his food. Happily, in recent years canine nutrition has been improved to such a degree that it has been attributed as one of the reasons dogs are now living longer than ever before.

Caution

Ignore those big brown eyes, begging you to let him finish the scraps on your plate. They can be high in calories and disrupt the nutritional balance of prepared pet food. Also, leftover bones can splinter and lodge inside your dog's digestive tract, causing pain and even death.

Water

The only thing your dog should be drinking is fresh, clean water. Milk contains lactose and can cause gastric upsets in dogs. Although some dogs love to drink from puddles, ponds and rivers, these may contain pollutants both chemical and natural, which might upset his stomach and can even be fatal. This is a particular hazard in warm weather when bacteria increase more rapidly.

Feeding puppies

Puppies are growing so quickly that they need two-and-a-half times more calories per unit of bodyweight than adult dogs, but also remember that they only have small stomachs so their food should be divided up into small feeds given several times a day (see page 85).

RESEARCH

Studies into the bone disorder rickets, which is associated with poor or unbalanced nutrition, show that the condition is now rarely if ever presented at veterinary surgeries. This is attributed to the widespread feeding of prepared pet food, which is formulated to contain all the nutrients dogs need for optimum health.

Supplements and additives

Everyone is more health conscious these days and that includes pet owners. Many worry that if they only took the time to prepare food specially for their dog he would be much happier. There are also concerns as to whether commercial pet foods might contain potentially harmful additives, and whether or not vitamin and mineral supplements are necessary.

With so many questions, and a range of answers from different pet food companies, it can be difficult to know what to do for the best. One thing is clear, however: unlike humans, dogs don't care about presentation or what their food looks like. It's the texture, smell and flavour that really excites them.

Give him a treat

You can feed your dog commercial pet food but still prepare him a delicious home-cooked meal using good cuts of meat and fish from time to time. Home-cooked meals are particularly appreciated if a dog is recovering from illness or surgery. Freshly cooked boiled rice and chicken fed in small amounts can be very palatable and is easily digested.

Supplements

- As a general rule, if you are feeding a complete, balanced pet food there should be no need to feed additional vitamin and mineral supplements to keep your dog happy and bouncing with good health.
- There is some evidence that an excess of minerals can be harmful to your dog and an overload of one mineral can deplete another.
- Dogs are natural carnivores and owners who put their dogs on a vegetarian diet can cause them health problems such as anaemia, so check with your vet about additional supplements before starting a meat-free regime.
- There is some evidence that fish oil may be beneficial to dogs with conditions such as arthritis, skin problems or wound infections.
- Always check with your vet before feeding any supplement to your dog.

Additives

Preservatives tend to be used in dried dog food, as the canning process itself helps to preserve wet food. This is why canned food should be disposed of within a day of opening and kept in the refrigerator with a lid on between feeds.

Pet food manufacturers may avoid additives but it is not always clear whether the ingredients they use already contain some. Not all additives are harmful and some may even be beneficial, but the long-term effects of some additives is not clear. It makes sense to avoid highly coloured food – your dog really won't worry that his food is a muddy brown colour!

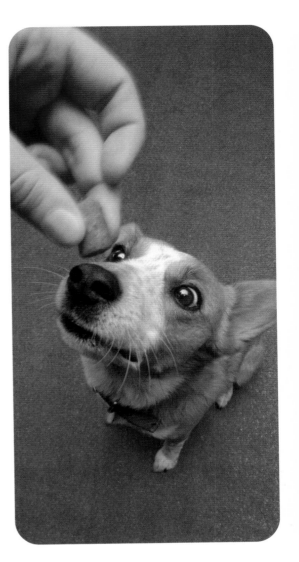

RESEARCH

Pet food manufacturers sponsor much of the research into the effects of commercial pet food on canine health so it can be difficult to find unbiased results into the effects of feeding home-made food. However, common sense will tell you there is a huge difference between feeding table scraps and cooking high-quality food specially for your dog.

Eating grass

You may notice that your dog often decides to supplement his diet by chewing mouthfuls of grass from your garden. It's not known exactly why some dogs like to eat grass, but it may be connected to a need for extra roughage. Grass is a natural emetic, so it's a good idea to keep your dog outside until he has been sick.

What a treat!

Here are some recipes that are guaranteed to make your dog extremely happy. Even though it takes a little time and effort to prepare these treats for him, it's an extremely satisfying thing to do.

Happy dog tip

Your dog will be extra-happy on a hot day if you offer him a home-made 'pupsicle'! Simply mix some chicken or beef gravy with water and freeze in ice-cube trays. For an extra treat, you could pop in a rawhide chew halfway through the freezing process.

You can save time in the future by cooking up large batches of treats and freezing any that you don't use immediately.

Happy cooking

To be on the safe side, cook all ingredients thoroughly. Although some owners advocate feeding raw food, there is no way of controlling the bacteria or chemicals in uncooked food. Be careful not to feed ingredients that are likely to give your dog an upset stomach: check out the list on page 11.

Get creative

Use your imagination to combine different ingredients into delicious high-value treats for your dog. Try liquidizing cooked liver, combining it with egg and a little flour and baking it into a cake, or combining a tin of tuna (in brine) with two eggs, a cup of wholemeal flour and a tablespoon of garlic powder. Liquify to the consistency of cake mix, spread onto a greased baking tray and bake at 180°C (gas mark 4) for 15–20 minutes, then cut into treat-sized squares.

Chocolate treats

For an extra-special treat at Easter or Christmas, melt down some doggy chocolate drops and set them in a fun-shaped mould. Simply place the drops in a heatproof bowl over a saucepan part-filled with water. Warm steadily, stirring until the chocolate melts. Lightly grease the mould and spoon in the mixture. If you are making an Easter egg, spread the mixture up over the sides of the mould to help join the two halves together. Place in the refrigerator to set. Put a couple of home-made or shop-bought dog biscuits inside one half, press the other half on top and spread the edges with more melted chocolate to seal.

Doggy stew

Make your dog a delicious stew using chicken and a selection of vegetables such as finely chopped carrot, runner beans, chopped celery and a cup of brown or white rice. Pour on water or chicken stock and bake in the oven at 180°C (gas mark 4) for about 45 minutes.

Happy dog biscuits

Ingredients

90 g (3 oz) wholemeal flour
15 g (½ oz) solid fat
3 stock cubes
2 tbsp grated cheese
1 litre (1½ pints) milk
50–75 ml (2–3 fl oz) stock or water

Method

Rub the flour and fat together. Crumble the stock cubes into the mixture and add the grated cheese. Add the milk and stock or water a little at a time, to form a stiff dough. Roll out and cut into squares. Place on a floured baking sheet and bake in the oven at 180°C (gas mark 4) for 45 minutes. Allow to cool and store in an airtight container.

Too much or too little?

Is your dog very fussy about what he eats? Or is he so greedy that he steals food from your plate when you're not looking? Food is such a staple of life that when we offer a meal to our dogs and they turn up their noses and refuse to eat, we can be left feeling guilty and frustrated, almost as if we've let them down in some way.

On the other hand, it can be very annoying if you are just about to sit down to lunch and turn your back for a moment, only to return and discover that your dog has helped himself! However, whatever the problem, there is always a solution.

> **Caution**
> With any eating problems, it is always advisable to take your dog to the vet so that any medical cause, such as changes to the dog's metabolic rate, can be ruled out.

Fussy eater

Owners who resort to spoon-feeding fussy eaters or constantly tempting them with different flavours and varieties of food, will actually be making the problem even worse.

To encourage your dog to eat, try putting down a daily allowance of balanced, complete food in a clean bowl. If he doesn't finish it, don't offer him anything else (particularly not snacks and treats), and just before you go to bed at night dispose of any food left in the bowl. Repeat this the following day and most behaviourists predict that you will see an improvement within a few days. Remember, you have his best interests at heart, so don't worry that you are being mean.

Bear in mind that a puppy will have growth spurts and his appetite will vary from time to time, so try not to worry too much.

Canine thief

Some dogs are very tempted by the smell of food and the best way to stop them thieving is to store all food away whenever they are unsupervised.

As dogs grow bigger, some get into the habit of standing on their back legs and investigating worktops in the kitchen – sometimes referred to as 'counter surfing'. Trying to interrupt this behaviour with loud noises or squirting from a water pistol can traumatize an anxious dog and

may not be the best solution. Instead, you could try sticking a strip of adhesive parcel tape or fly paper along the edge of the worktop: the dog will put his paws on this and associate the behaviour with something that feels unpleasant. You will have to change the sticky tape or paper on a daily basis, but within a couple of weeks he should lose interest in this behaviour.

If your dog persists in trying to steal food, put him in another room while you are eating or preparing food. Seek the advice of your vet, or ask for a referral to a professional animal behaviour consultant for management tips.

The happy mouth dog

By the time your puppy is six weeks old he will have all 28 of his 'baby' (milk) teeth. The adult teeth have usually come through by the time the dog is between four and six months old.

As with a baby, you can make your teething puppy happier during this uncomfortable phase by providing him with lots of tough, safe toys and chews on which to work his teeth and gums. Your vet will check his teeth at his annual check-up and may advise professional teeth cleaning, but in the meantime you can help him stay a 'happy mouth' dog by learning how to brush his teeth.

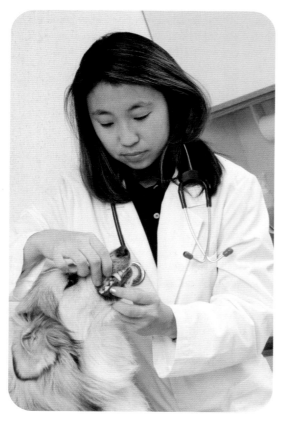

Why brush?

Brushing your dog's teeth is the best way you can help to prevent gum disease. It's important to do this, because if your dog has untreated gum disease the bacteria that cause the inflammation can enter the bloodstream and may cause or aggravate problems with other organs such as the heart, liver and kidneys.

How to brush

If you have a puppy, you can accustom him to having his mouth and teeth handled from an early age. Check for broken teeth and that the adult teeth are coming through when his baby teeth have fallen out.

Put on a rubber glove or a special tooth-cleaning tip and gently rub your finger over your dog's gums and teeth. Put a tiny blob of pet toothpaste on your finger and rub this over his teeth. You can gradually get him used to having his teeth brushed with a pet toothbrush. For effective cleaning, do this a couple of times a week.

Chewing problems

Ask family members to tidy up their toys, socks, slippers and so on, so that your puppy can't chew them. Provide him with firm, non-crumbly dog chews and toys on which to work his baby teeth. He may also enjoy gnawing at a carrot or celery stick. Avoid giving your dog bones to gnaw on as they can splinter and get stuck in his throat.

RESEARCH

85 per cent of dogs over three years of age show signs of gum disease. Plaque gradually accumulates on the teeth. If allowed to build up, it combines with minerals in the saliva and hardens into a substance called tartar (scale). If plaque and tartar are not removed by your vet it causes painful, foul-smelling inflammatory gum disease (gingivitis).

Signs of a sore mouth

Your dog could be experiencing problems with his teeth or gums if he:

- Is eating his food gingerly, using only one side of his mouth or if he picks at his food.
- Loses weight because it's painful for him to eat.
- Is pawing at his mouth.
- Is drooling excessively.
- Has halitosis (bad breath).

Seek veterinary advice for any of the above symptoms, and especially if you find a broken tooth or his gums are raw and bleeding.

Happy dog tip

Feeding your dog dry food and providing special teeth cleaning canine chews can help to keep his mouth and teeth healthy.

Fat dogs are not happy dogs

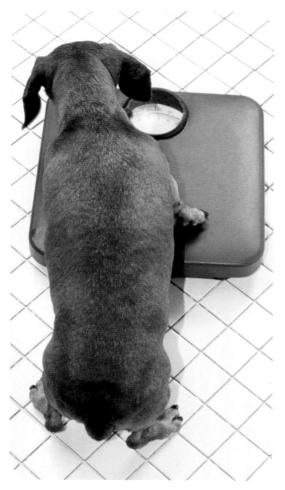

If you take your dog for an annual check-up, his weight will be assessed and your vet can tell you if he is piling on the pounds. This is definitely not a happy situation, but thankfully it can be remedied.

Doggy diet tips

Many veterinary surgeries run weight-management clinics for pets, but if you prefer to work alone there are a few dieting guidelines you should try to follow:

- Avoid giving food treats as rewards, as these can soon build up extra calories. Use verbal praise, toys and play instead.
- Give him more exercise. Relying on food deprivation will make your dog very unhappy.
- Look for food that is high in fibre and low in fat. Your vet can prescribe canine diet food if necessary.
- Be realistic about how much weight you expect your dog to lose. As with humans, a slow, steady weight loss is better than a rapid one.
- Don't try fad dog diets. They are nutritionally unbalanced and will deprive your pet of the essential vitamins and minerals he needs for optimal health.
- Don't forget that your dog may slow down and exercise less as he grows older, so you will need to make adjustments to his calorie intake.

Is he fat?

A healthy canine body should look as if it is in proportion. You should be able to feel your dog's ribs and not see visible folds of fat. If he is too fat, you will not able to see his waist and his tail will look and feel thick.

If your dog is overweight he could suffer from serious health problems including arthritis, diabetes, heart disease, kidney disease and respiratory problems. He may also be lethargic, sleep more and ultimately have a shorter lifespan.

> **Happy dog tip**
> Don't give in to begging. While your dog is dieting, try putting him in another room while you prepare and eat your food. This way, you won't be tempted to give him titbits.

It takes two

Chances are that if your dog is overweight from overeating and lack of exercise, you will be too. Why not join him in a weight-loss programme by slimming together and increasing your exercise regime so that you both adopt healthier lifestyles and become fitter and happier?

Party time

During certain holiday periods, such as Christmas or Thanksgiving, we can all become prone to over-indulgence. However, make sure everyone in your family understands and sticks to your dog's diet or all the hard work can quickly be undone. If you can't resist giving him treats, provide some low-calorie ones such as carrot sticks (surprisingly, lots of dogs love these) or rawhide chews.

'More dogs than ever are classed as overweight'

7 Exercise

Exercising with your dog really is one of the joys of ownership and the best way you and he can enjoy time together. Although the thought of taking him out for a walk on a cold, dark morning may not seem a great idea, it will help to keep you both healthy and is a vital part of his daily routine.

Try to think up different routes and get to know other dog owners, so your walk becomes a happy and sociable start to your day. Remember that, as long as your dog is getting enough exercise for his size and type (see pages 40–41), what you do when you're out with your dog is more important than the amount of time you both spend outdoors. This chapter will give you plenty of ideas for fun activities that will help to keep your dog happy and enthusiastic about your life together.

Take care
Be careful not to over-exert a young puppy. If he looks tired when you're out walking, stop for a few minutes to give him a rest. Don't get into the habit of picking him up and carrying him home, though – you could regret this by the time he's fully grown!

Weather watch
Whatever outdoor activities you choose to undertake, you will need to keep your eye on the weather if your dog is to benefit both physically and mentally, and enjoy his exercise times to the full. Older dogs and those with fine, short hair will appreciate wearing a warm, cosy dog coat when they are outside on cold, wet days. Exercising in hot weather can cause a dog to overheat, so always carry a water bottle with you and take regular breaks so that you can offer him a drink.

If you suspect your dog is overheating, hose him down for about ten minutes, paying special attention to underneath his belly – the coat is finer there and your dog will cool down faster. Seek urgent veterinary attention if his breathing does not quickly return to normal.

Let's play!

Playing games with your dog is a great opportunity for you both to learn to communicate, trust, have fun and work together. There are hundreds of things you can do in a non-competitive environment that can help with training and will also keep your dog stimulated.

Playing games will significantly increase the bond between the two of you and is good exercise too. You can enjoy playing with your dog on his own, or invite some of his canine friends and their owners to join in the fun as well. It is important to consider your dog's age, health and physical abilities before you ask him to play any games. Some dogs are so enthusiastic they will carry on playing for too long and risk injury.

Toy time
Collect a variety of toys for your dog and give each of them a name. You can then use a clicker and some food treats (see pages 74–75) to help teach your dog to identify and pick the toys up in his mouth, either giving them to you or dropping them into a toy box.

Always carry some toys in your pocket when out on a walk with your dog, so that you can use them in a game. It's particularly useful to be able to engage him in play when you see distractions ahead, such as another dog. Balls, Frisbees and tug-of-war toys are ideal.

Games you can play

Hide and seek Put your dog in the down and stay position (see pages 76–79) then go off and hide. Call his name and see how long he takes to find you. Praise him every time he is successful.

Treasure hunt You can play this indoors or out. Hide some treats or toys then release your dog to go off and find them. Make it easy for him at first, then increase the difficulty by hiding treats under cushions or furniture, or in another room.

Follow the leader Set up an obstacle course using items such as cones, steps, a shallow paddling pool, a hula hoop, a small jump and so on. Time how quickly you and your dog can successfully negotiate the course. You can play this game with your dog on or off the lead.

Showjumping Set up a mini course of showjumps for you and your dog to jump around. Use things that will fall down easily if your dog knocks them: try putting the handle of a mop or a broom across two chairs or upturned buckets but keep the height low so that there is no risk to your dog's joints. Children love playing this energetic game.

Find it Line up several empty containers in a row. Place a treat underneath one of them. See how long it takes your dog to find the 'winning' tub.

Balancing Ask your dog to walk across a plank balanced between two buckets. Start with one that is quite wide and gradually reduce this down to a narrow plank. Remember that this is a balancing game, not a circus high-wire act, so keep the plank low to the ground to avoid injuries.

Tug of war Some trainers advise against playing tug-of-war games, but provided you ensure that it is you and not the dog that remains in charge at all times, and you are able safely to signal the end of the game, they can be fun. It's best to avoid using items of clothing such as an old jumper, as this could encourage your dog to pull at something you are wearing. Instead, make a toy from knotting thick rope, or invest in one of the many tug-of-war style toys available in pet stores.

'Always ensure that children are safely supervised when they are playing with dogs'

Get walking

Walks are often nowhere near as much fun for the owner as they are for the dog. You trudge the same route every day and see the same sights – and the only time you interact with your dog is to reprimand him for barking or when you try to put him back on the lead. It needn't be like this!

Walking your dog is an excellent way to develop your relationship and improve his social skills. Dogs love exercise and enjoy spending this quality time with their 'pack leader'.

Ways to make walks fun

Variety is the key to keeping both you and your dog happy, so if you're finding dog-walking a chore try some of these ideas:

Vary the route If you're bored then your dog probably is too. Remember that he will pick up on your moods. If you live near a park, nature reserve or beach, get into the car and take him there. You could resolve to make one dog-walk a week a special outing involving the whole family.

Visit shops and friends Combine the walk with errands such as shopping or a visit to the bank. If you have friends who are dog owners, arrange to meet up and walk together so the dogs can play.

Take some exercise Jogging with your dog will keep you both fit and he will enjoy it. Cycling while your dog trots alongside can also be fun.

Play Frisbee Visit the park and see how far you can throw a Frisbee with your dog catching it before it hits the ground.

Explore new places This might be a street you haven't walked before or a new route by the river.

Make new friends You will soon recognize people and dogs if you walk regularly. Dogs help to break the ice so new friendships may develop.

Get educational Agility and obedience training mean exercise for you and training for your pet.

Routes to understanding

If you have a puppy or a rescue dog it's important to get him used to as many different situations as possible as each provides its own lessons:

Park Learns to socialize with other pets and curious children.

Countryside Learns not to chase, and possibly scare, livestock and wildlife.

Town Learns to deal with busy streets and noise.

Friends' and relatives' houses Learns to relax with other people and their pets.

Beach Discovers sand and water, the fun of digging and splashing in the sea.

Different types of transport Learns to behave well on noisy trains and buses.

School gates Learns to be patient while receiving lots of attention from children, and how to greet other 'family pack' members.

Happy walking do's...

✔ Take food treats and toys along to break up the routine.

✔ Ask different family members to walk the dog so that he bonds with all of you.

✔ Walk in all kinds of weather conditions (see page 99) so that he isn't frightened of wind or hail.

✔ Allow extra walking time for young, working breeds, such as Border Collies, to help put their energy to good use.

✔ Be a responsible owner and take a poop scoop or bags with you.

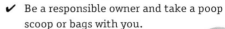

... and don'ts

✗ Don't throw sticks or stones for your dog to chase. Sticks can splinter in his throat and swallowed stones may cause blockages, which often have to be removed surgically.

✗ Never chase your dog if he runs off – he'll think it's a great game and will revel in the attention. Instead, work on the recall command. Praise him when he returns, and give him a toy or treat so that he realizes coming back to you is more rewarding.

✗ Don't reprimand your dog for scenting. This is a natural reaction to new territory.

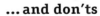

Agility

Agility is a fantastic sport for dogs and owners of all ages to enjoy. It is one of the fastest growing sports in the UK, Western Europe and the USA. Using voice and hand signals, handlers are timed as they instruct their dogs to negotiate a series of obstacles such as tunnels, jumps and ramps.

If you've done some basic obedience work with your dog (see Chapter 5), you can take this to another level by having a go at agility training.

Can any dog do it?

Any dog – cross-breed, mongrel or pedigree – can take part provided he is over 12 months old, and is reasonably fit and healthy. Before starting any agility training, have a chat with your vet to ensure your dog is physically capable as the sport involves running at speed, jumping hurdles, balancing and negotiating various obstacles.

There are elementary, starter and novice classes available for dogs of all sizes including minis (dogs under 38 cm (15 in) high at the withers). There are also classes for young handlers, seniors and disabled participants.

Joining a class

Agility is so popular that you shouldn't have to travel far to find a group of enthusiasts who will help you and your dog learn more about this exciting sport. Watch a couple of sessions first to see what is involved and help you decide whether you would like to try. Joining a class will ensure you have access to proper equipment and tuition, and it's a great way for you and your dog to socialize with other dogs and their owners.

Obstacles

You can expect to see:
- Hurdles to jump over.
- Hoops and tyres to jump through.
- Long jump.
- Pipe tunnels and collapsible tunnels.
- A-ramp.
- Seesaw.
- Weaving poles.

Some of the obstacles have coloured areas painted on them that your dog must touch with his paws as he moves along them.

Perfect timing

In a competition, dogs will tackle a course of up to 20 obstacles. Each round is timed, with the fastest clear round winning. Penalties are incurred for errors such as missing out an obstacle, knocking one down or failing to touch the 'contact' points. However, it's not always the fastest dog that wins: quite often a slow, steady clear round will beat a speedy, less accurate effort.

> **RESEARCH**
> Studies show that it is the speed at which a dog travels and the force with which he hits an obstacle, rather than the height of a jump, that causes most injuries in agility. Although it is fun watching your dog go as fast as he possibly can, make sure he's not going so fast that he is likely to hurt himself.

> **Happy dog tip**
> Even if you don't go to agility training classes, you can have fun by setting up a mini obstacle course for you and your dog to negotiate.

What do you need?

- Sensible, non-slip trainers.
- Waist bag full of treats to use as rewards.
- Non-baggy clothing so that your dog can see your hand signals clearly.
- Visor or baseball cap to help you keep the sun out of your eyes and enable you to see all parts of the agility course.
- Some trainers like to use a harness to help their dog balance when training him to negotiate contact obstacles.

'It's not always the fastest dog that wins'

Flyball

If your dog has lots of energy, enjoys romping around and can fetch and retrieve, then he is going to love flyball. This thrilling international sport involves competitive relay racing for teams of four dogs and their owners. It's fast, furious and above all fantastic fun for everyone involved, including the spectators.

RESEARCH
Studies show that exercise during the incubation period of an infection may worsen the prognosis, so if your dog is ill or recovering from illness don't force him to participate in exhaustive exercise activities, such as agility training or flyball (see pages 104–105).

Flyball began in the 1970s and is now enjoyed in countries all over the world including the USA, Canada, Japan, Australia, the UK and many parts of Europe. Give it a try!

What is it?

Each dog in the team runs a short course over four low box hurdles. When he reaches the end, he triggers a box that releases a tennis ball, which he has to catch and then run back to the starting line with the ball in his mouth. As soon as the first dog returns the next one can go. The winning team is the first to get four dogs and four balls back successfully, without any faults. The most common faults are dropping a ball, and missing out or going around one of the hurdles.

Can any dog do it?

Any breed and size of dog can participate in flyball, as it is the shortest dog on the team that determines the size of the hurdles. All dogs must be at least 12 months, and usually 18 months of age, to compete in a tournament.

Dogs must be quite fit as this is a vigorous exercise, but it is an excellent way for them to burn off lots of energy and very useful for bored dogs that could otherwise develop destructive behaviour patterns.

Two's company

As well as teams of four dogs, selected from a squad of six, there are occasional fun events such as pairs and starters. There are several categories:

Open Any two dogs together.

Mixed Any two dogs of different breeds, including cross-breeds and mongrels.

Mini-maxi One standard dog and one small dog.

Starters Young dogs (12 months and over) and new and inexperienced dogs. There can be some hilarious outcomes for dogs learning the basics – one owner reported that her dog retrieved the ball and then ran off to a nearby lake for a quick swim, before returning to finish the course.

Points

Dogs competing in tournaments affiliated to recognized flyball associations gain points, which accumulate and eventually earn the dog certificates, medals and awards.

Getting started

Your national canine association or the internet are good places to start looking for a flyball club near you. Watch a couple of events and have a chat with some of the enthusiasts you will find there, to help you decide if the sport is for you and your dog. Flyball is a lot of fun and is held indoors and outdoors, at all times of year.

Heelwork to music

If you are quite creative, love music and enjoy dancing, you might like to try the relatively new sport of heelwork to music. This is now extremely popular all over the world and has evolved into many different divisions including musical dressage, heelwork and freestyle.

Handlers may wear costumes and use some props, while dogs can wear fancy collars. Most dogs really enjoy dancing to music and it's fun trying to find a composition that suits your dog's personality and the way he moves.

Can any dog do this?

Yes: a dog of any breed or size, pedigree or cross-breed, can have fun with heelwork to music. If you don't want to compete, you can entertain your family and friends. Some people get pleasure from taking dogs to perform for senior citizens or at a children's home (see pages 110–111).

Enthusiasm and confidence are much more important elements of the performance than the

> ### Happy dog tip
> Regardless of whether you want to train your dog in a heelwork routine, you can still put on some music, start dancing around the room and invite your dog to join you – he'll think it's great fun! Marching music has a great beat for beginners.

degree of difficulty in your routine. You can make the work as energetic or as elegant as you wish, and develop moves that specifically suit your dog's abilities.

What training is involved?

Your dog must have some basic obedience training. He must be able to:

- Walk off the lead in the heelwork position without becoming distracted by lights, music and other dogs.
- Sit.
- Stay.
- Down.
- Wait.
- Recall.

All the right moves

Freestyle routines (where the dog doesn't have to be in the heelwork position throughout) are very popular, as they allow for more creativity. Fun moves you will see include:

- Walking on back legs.
- Creeping.
- Jumping through hoops or outstretched arms.
- Weaving through handler's legs.
- Rollovers.
- High fives (where the dog reaches up with his paw to touch the handler's hand).
- Playing dead.
- Reversing around handler.

Getting started

If your local dog training club does not offer classes in heelwork to music, they may be able to recommend a trainer who specializes in this sport. If not, contact one of the many associated organizations – the internet is an excellent source of information on national and international heelwork to music organizations. Attend an event or training workshop to find out what's involved. There are also books and videos available to help you get started.

What will I need?

- Portable CD player.
- Comfortable non-slip shoes.
- Most handlers train in trousers, as this is easier for the dog if he is learning some of the more complex moves such as leg weaving.
- A sense of humour.

Competitions

Competitive classes are available for all abilities, from beginners to advanced. They are judged on degree of technical difficulty, the dog's willingness to work, the partnership between dog and handler, and how well the music is interpreted. Some experienced handlers are able to compete with up to six dogs in a single routine, which can last for several minutes.

At your service

Another fun way of exercising your dog and providing him with mental and physical stimulation is to encourage him to do a little bit of community service. If your dog is never happier than when he's being petted by people, you might like to consider taking advantage of his good nature and giving a few hours of your time back to the community.

Senior citizens in residential homes are often delighted to receive a visit from a canine friend and dogs are always instant ice-breakers, so no-one is ever stuck for words. You can help bring a real high point to someone's day simply by visiting them with your dog.

Can any dog do it?

For this job, temperament is much more important than breed. A good therapy dog will be:

- Sociable.
- Calm.
- Friendly.
- Polite (he won't push himself towards people he's not been invited to approach).
- Obedient.
- Willing to interact.

Therapy dogs

It's very important that the right dogs are used for therapy. Potential therapy dogs will undergo an assessment of their temperament and behaviour. They must also have been in the ownership of the handler for a specified length of time, so that a good bond exists between them, and references are usually required.

Once a dog has passed all the tests, he is usually issued with a special, easily identifiable coat and lead, and an area coordinator will arrange placements for him. Just an hour a week on a regular basis can really make a difference.

Where dogs can help

Community service dogs regularly visit:

- Hospitals.
- Care homes.
- Children's homes.
- Schools.
- Prisons.
- Youth groups.
- Hospices.

Will it make my dog happy?

Definitely, but only if your dog likes going to different places and meeting a variety of people. This type of dog will enjoy all the fuss and attention, and view it as a positive experience that he will enjoy repeating each week. As the owner, you will get the satisfaction of seeing the dog that makes you feel so happy work his magic on everyone else.

If your dog tends to become anxious or fearful among strangers, don't push him into undertaking therapy visits as he will almost certainly find it stressful and overwhelming.

Getting started

Contact one of the organizations that specialize in pets as therapy (often referred to as animal-assisted therapy) for more information and details of their acceptance procedures.

RESEARCH

Studies show that dogs can be very good for your health. Stroking a dog or even just being in the same room with him can help to lower blood pressure, speed recovery from illness and bring a sense of calm. Researchers have also found that dogs used as pets in therapy groups can help relieve the symptoms of mental health problems such as schizophrenia. The non-judgemental, unconditional love given by dogs helps people to connect with them and express feelings that they would otherwise be unable to acknowledge. It's official: happy dogs can make happy people.

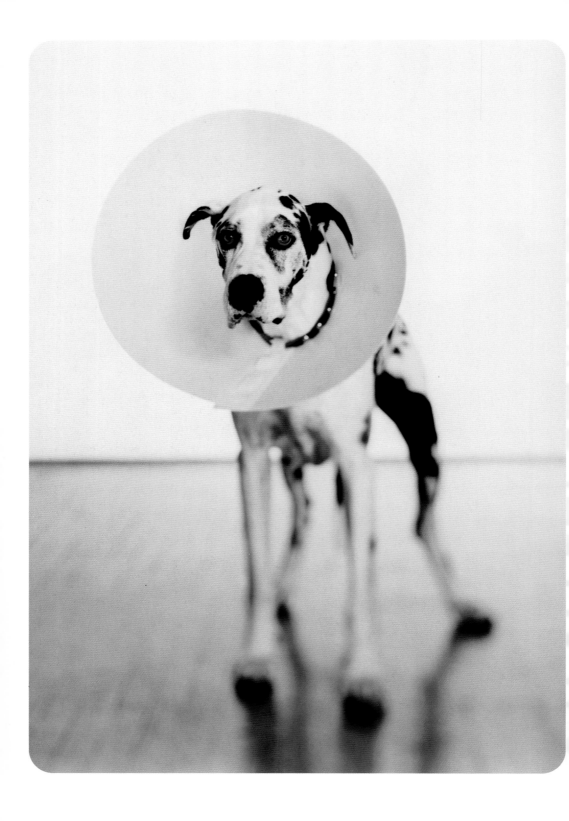

8 Vets, pets and scary stuff

All loving owners want to keep their dog happy, but unfortunately there are plenty of scary things that could take the wag right out of his tail. However, it's not difficult to help your dog through situations he finds scary. This chapter will show you what to do.

Every dog is unique and what scares one may not affect another at all. The more that your dog has been socialized and introduced to different people, pets, situations and environments as a puppy, the less likely he will be to develop any phobias or anxieties as an adult.

Scary stuff
Things that might make your dog unhappy include:
- Visiting the vet.
- Strangers, children, crowds.
- Other pets.
- Moving house.
- Travelling.
- Loud noises.

Some dogs have very specific but apparently random things that terrify them, such as people wearing hats or carrying umbrellas.

Signs of stress
Obvious signs that your dog might be stressed include:
- Excessive panting or drooling.
- Licking of lips.
- Trembling.
- Immobility as if frozen to the spot.
- Urinating.
- Whining.
- Barking, growling or snapping.
- Lying down.
- Rolling over.
- Flattened ears.
- Pacing, inability to sleep or rest.
- Destructive behaviour, such as chewing or scratching.
- Trying to hide behind things.
- Showing whites of his eyes.
- Tail clamped down very low, wagging weakly.
- Anorexia.

How to help
Try to figure out what is upsetting your dog and then treat the cause of the problem, rather than the symptoms. In the short term, try distracting him with a treat, toy or verbal reassurance. Turn him away, take him for a short walk and then encourage him to have a quiet nap. Sleep deprivation is just as debilitating for dogs as it is for humans and can cause much stress.

Find a dog-friendly vet

There will always be things in life that we find less enjoyable than others, and for a dog a trip to the vet will probably come pretty high on his list. Unfortunately for him, visiting the vet is a fact of life that can't be avoided and it's important that it does not become a stressful situation.

You do not want every visit to the vet to leave you and your dog feeling anxious and exhausted by the trauma of it all. So, how can you make going to the vet a fun experience for your pet?

Sign up

If you have a puppy and your veterinary surgery holds puppy socialization classes, it's a good idea to enrol for these. Such classes provide an excellent opportunity to begin creating positive associations with the staff and the surgery itself, as they involve fun, games, attention and usually lots of treats and toys.

Some surgeries also run adolescent or senior dog clinics once or twice a year, at which dogs in these life stages are given a thorough health check. These are useful opportunities for helping your dog to overcome his anxieties.

'Don't reward nervous behaviour with extra attention'

If your dog is vet phobic

- Ask other dog owners to recommend a vet who is prepared to spend time and be extra-patient with nervous dogs.
- Visit the surgery and have a chat with the staff to get advice. If they seem dismissive of you, find another surgery.
- Ask whether an appointment system exists, so that your dog can be seen at times when the surgery is less busy.
- Visit the surgery often, even when your dog is not due to be seen. Begin by taking him there, putting him on the lead and walking around the car park, if there is one. Ask the staff if you can go inside and sit in the waiting room for a few minutes. If possible, ask a vet or nurse to give your dog a particularly high-value treat (which you've taken with you) and make a fuss of him before you leave. Your aim is to take the fear out of the situation so that your dog begins to associate the surgery with positive experiences.
- Whenever you visit the surgery, take some treats and a toy with you, so that you are able to give your dog lots of attention in the waiting room and distract him from becoming worried.
- Try to remain calm yourself and don't reward his nervous behaviour with extra attention. Act normally and speak to him in a calm, happy and reassuring voice.

If your dog remains terrified of going to the surgery and you feel you can't cope, ask your vet for further advice. They may recommend giving the dog a very light sedative to relax him just before his visit.

Happy dog tip
Some surgeries use plug-in dog-appeasing pheromone (DAP) diffusers to help a nervous dog feel calm. The pheromones signal to the dog that he is safe and secure. If your dog is very worried, you could ask your surgery if they are able to do this.

RESEARCH
New research could have massive implications for the treatment of fear and stress problems. Scientists have discovered distinct laughs for rats, chimpanzees and dogs. Although a dog laugh is not easily heard by humans (to the untrained ear it sounds like panting), dogs that hear their own distinctive laugh are soon put into a good mood. In a study, when the sound of a dog's laugh was piped into a kennel or shelter, the mood of the dogs immediately brightened and they began playing.

Happy families

If you are an animal lover and already have dogs and other pets, you probably have dreams of them all getting on well in one big, happy family. It can be very upsetting when things don't go to plan and your new dog is either fearful of your other pets or aggressive towards them.

The key to all your dogs and other pets getting on with each other is to take lots of time during the initial introduction stage.

Happy dog tip

Ensure that everyone in the family continues to make just as much fuss of the existing dog as they always have done, so that he doesn't feel threatened or insecure. Keep to his normal feeding and exercising routines.

Pleased to meet you

If your new and existing dogs are both neutered and have been well socialized, you should experience few problems when they meet. Introducing an entire male or female into a household will increase the risk of aggression, territory marking and other antisocial behaviours.

If your existing dog has lived alone with you for several years and had little contact with other dogs, then it is asking a lot of him to accept a newcomer. The stress that this will cause may be too much, and he will become very unhappy as a result. It may be better to postpone your decision to get a second dog, as it is not worth bringing misery on the one you've already got.

Puppy love

You can introduce the idea of a new puppy into your house before he actually arrives. Simply take a towel or blanket to the breeder and rub it over the puppy, then bring it home and put it somewhere your existing dog can find it easily and smell it. Don't put it in his bed, though, as he will find this very unsettling!

Similarly, you can rub a towel over your existing dog and take it along to the new puppy, so that he becomes familiar with the scent.

New arrivals

- Arrange to introduce the dogs outside, on neutral territory. Enlist the help of a friend, or someone else your dog does not view as part of his pack, to pick up your new dog.
- Keep both dogs on leads as you allow them to meet, greet and sniff each other.
- Keep your interactions with both your dogs low key, and try not to make more of a fuss of one than the other.
- Reward calm behaviour with verbal praise and attention, then set off for a walk together.
- Keep the dogs on leads, but other than this try to intervene as little as possible between them.
- Never leave the animals unattended until they have bonded completely.
- When you get home, if you have an indoor kennel or crate put the new dog in it,

Meet the cat

Follow the same basic principles when your dog first meets your cat. Always keep him on a lead, and make use of an indoor crate until both pets realize that they can safely smell and see each other without fear of being attacked.

particularly when the dogs are unsupervised or when you go to bed. This will give the dog outside the kennel a safe opportunity to smell, see and get used to the newcomer. After a while, swap the dogs over so that the new dog gets a chance to explore.

- At mealtimes, feed your existing dog first so that he maintains his position as pack leader.

Bang bang!

Many dogs are terrified by loud, unexpected bangs from fireworks or thunderstorms. They become extremely stressed, and will hide, run away, or run to their owners, and possibly pant, whine and show other symptoms of extreme stress and anxiety.

It is very upsetting for an owner to see their dog this unhappy and many feel frustrated that there is nothing they can do to comfort him. The good news is that vets have been working hard on this problem and have come up with some innovative ideas to help solve it.

Hearing check

Even a normally confident dog can be changed into a trembling nervous wreck when faced with the unexpected sound of loud fireworks or a sudden storm. If this is the case with your dog, begin by getting his hearing checked by your vet. It's important to find out whether he has sensitive hearing or any significant hearing loss, which means a loud noise will make him jump.

If your dog has normal hearing, then his fear is behavioural and there are several things you can do to try to put the wag back in his tail.

Sound-sensitive CDs

CDs are now available specifically for pets that are frightened of fireworks or thunderstorms. Play the CD very quietly at first, while the dog is doing something pleasurable such as eating his dinner or playing a game with you. Over several weeks, gradually turn up the volume, so that he gets used to the noise of thunder or fireworks and begins to develop pleasant associations with it (such as food and toys).

You should be aware that sound CDs can only help a dog get used to the noise and cannot replicate the changes in air pressure, light flashes and smells that accompany a real storm or firework display.

DAPs

Plugging in a dog-appeasing pheromone (DAP) diffuser (see page 34) may help to relax your dog. The problem is that you cannot always predict when a storm or fireworks are going to start. However, if you do know, pull the curtains or blinds in one room, put on some background music to fill the silence between bangs and activate the diffuser. Then, very importantly, try to ignore your dog.

I'm frightened!

It's a natural reaction to want to comfort your dog when he's afraid, but in doing so you could be making the situation worse because the dog may think you are praising him for showing signs of anxiety. After all, when you like what he's doing you tell him he's a good boy, speak to him in a special tone of voice, stroke him and give him cuddles, and he has no way of differentiating between praise for good behaviour and comfort for anxiety. If your dog wants to hide under your chair while the storm is going on, just ignore him and allow him to do this. Only pay attention to him when he is coping well. This way, you will make him a lot happier in the end.

RESEARCH

Studies show that the use of DAPs and CD sound recordings *together* appears to be the most effective way of tackling a dog's fear of loud noises. Owners who used both noted the dogs sought their owners less, became less vigilant and restless, and salivated less. The use of tranquillizers was not an effective solution to the long-term problem.

Safe haven

Dogs are at their happiest when they are settled into a routine, but unfortunately there are times when we are forced to disrupt their everyday peace and quiet. Family parties or celebrations, building work and redecorating can all play havoc with a dog's life.

Happy dog tip
Tell any children in your family that your dog's crate is his den and not an extra playroom for them! This is to be a place of sanctuary, just for your dog.

If you have done your best to socialize your dog properly since he was a puppy, you should not encounter too many problems. However, if you are uncertain of your dog's history or he has a naturally sensitive personality, crate training can help him to feel happy and safe.

Crate training

By getting your puppy or young dog used to an indoor kennel or crate, you will be providing him with a safe den to which he can escape and which he sees as a place of peace and calm. It is also possible to crate train an older dog, but be aware that it may take a little longer.

- Position the crate in a draught-free corner of the room where the dog can see you.
- Make the crate as comfortable as possible, filling it with a warm blanket, a bowl of water and some fun chew toys for him to gnaw at.
- Introduce the crate by leaving the door open and throwing some treats and toys inside to encourage the dog to go in and investigate.
- Play games with your dog in and around the crate and build up lots of positive associations with this 'security bunker'.
- You can place a blanket over the top of the crate to block out light and encourage him to nap.
- When you eventually close the door of the crate, make sure you have put lots of treat-filled toys in there and only leave your dog inside for short periods of time.

- If he is whining or barking, don't open the door. If you do, he will learn that these actions cause you to let him out and he will be encouraged to repeat the behaviour, rather than to stop it.
- Train your dog to settle in his crate both when you are in the room and when you have left it.
- Always remember that the crate is going to be your dog's safe haven – not a prison to restrain him or somewhere you send him when he has done something you don't like.

Reaping the benefits

The benefits of crate training are that when a potentially stressful situation arises, you can put your dog in his den and he will feel safe and happy. Do not leave him unattended in the crate for longer than three hours before taking him out for a walk to allow him to move, play and, of course, toilet.

Most dogs will not soil in their crate, which can be very useful if you have a housetraining problem, as you can take him straight outside to relieve himself when he wakes up.

Beating baby blues

Congratulations: you are proud new parents. The little bundle of joy you're bringing home has transformed your world. But how will the other family members adjust to the new arrival?

While you are absorbed by your newborn, your dog may feel jealous and resentful of the attention you're giving a new member of the 'family pack'. Helping your dog to adjust to this change is vital if you want to maintain a happy household.

Naturally, your baby will demand the majority of your time and affection. However, sooner or later you will have to ensure your dog happily accepts his new position in the family group. This can be done smoothly by following these suggestions:

Prenatal prep

Build up a routine for walking, feeding and playing with your dog. It's important not to unsettle him by disrupting this routine after the birth.

Make sure your pet is up to date with his jabs and wormer treatments. You're unlikely to have too much time for such things when the baby comes home.

Buy an indoor kennel or crate so that your pet has a special refuge if the noise and disturbance gets too much for him.

Dog meets baby

If your dog is well trained, ask him to sit and wait. Bring the baby over to him and encourage the dog to sniff around the cot. Dogs are inquisitive and your pet will want to smell the baby. Encourage this but don't allow him to get too close. Repeat this over a few short sessions until he is no longer curious. Make sure there is another adult present who can take the dog away if he reacts badly.

Reward calm behaviour with praise, treats or toys, but don't admonish the dog for bad behaviour – he mustn't associate the new baby with punishment.

Adjusting to family life

Once you have brought your baby home, it's important that you keep to your dog's routine and praise his good behaviour around the infant.

Don't leave your dog alone with the baby. Putting a screen door on your baby's room is a good idea, as it allows the dog to hear and smell the newcomer without getting too close.

'Is this a new animal in my territory?'

Try to involve your dog in all family outings. Soon he will accept that the infant has become part of his regular routine.

Who is the new arrival?

Your dog will use his nose foremost in investigating the newcomer.

'This is a new smell.'
'Is this a new animal in my territory?'

He will see you cuddling the new baby.

'The pack leader is holding the new creature.'
'This must be a new member of the pack.'

With praise for good behaviour, he will accept the new family member without jealousy.

'Welcome packmate!'

RESEARCH

Studies show that toy breeds, such as King Charles Spaniels and Pekingese, take three times longer to adjust to change in their family environment than working pastoral breeds, such as Collies and German Shepherds. This is because of their breeding as companion dogs, which makes them fiercely faithful to their owners. However, even toy breeds can adjust to a new baby and some become very protective of them.

Baby meets dog

As your infant grows, so will his curiosity. A dog is a wonderfully strange creature that merits investigation. Your baby will want to grab his tail, prod his fur and press that wet, sniffy nose. A successfully socialized dog will accept such forceful affection and even enjoy the attention. It's important that you encourage interaction, but supervise carefully. An over-excited dog may scare the baby, while a stray finger in the dog's eye will scare the dog.

Happy moving

There are few things more stressful in life than moving to a new home, and a sensitive dog can find this experience particularly difficult. After all, you are taking him away from a place with which he has many happy associations, and he will find it difficult to understand why he shouldn't return there.

To help things run smoothly, there are several sensible steps you can take before, during and after the move.

Change of address
- Get some new identity tags for your dog, engraved with details of your new address or telephone number. Swap these as soon as you arrive at the new house.
- If your dog is microchipped, inform the company holding the database of your change of address.
- Ask your veterinary surgery to update their records with your new details.

Pack up and go
Some dogs find it quite unsettling to see their owners packing away the contents of their home. You could ask a friend or neighbour with whom he is familiar to take him for a long walk and a visit to their house while you are packing, or you can help your dog feel safe by putting him in a quiet room or in his crate. The kitchen is often a good choice, as this is usually the last place to be emptied.

Pack up your dog's toys, bedding and food bowls last of all and get them out again as soon as you get to the new house. If possible, refrain from washing bedding for a couple of weeks, so that the dog is comforted by familiar smells. Consider plugging in a dog-appeasing pheromone (DAP) diffuser (see page 34) before, during and after moving to help him relax.

If you are moving a considerable distance, don't feed your dog for 12 hours prior to travelling. If he

suffers from travel sickness, your vet can prescribe some medication to help him.

Put your dog in a travel crate or special dog harness (which secures to the seatbelt fixings) and stop frequently for water and toilet breaks.

On arrival

When you arrive at the new house, confine the dog to one room or put him in his crate, with his unwashed bedding and some of his toys. There will be plenty of time for him to explore later on. Allowing him to roam around when there are removal men present can risk escape or injury.

Before letting your dog outside, check the garden fence and gates thoroughly to make sure there are no gaps through which he can escape.

Unpack as much as possible before letting your dog out, so that he can immediately see and smell familiar things. If your dog is anxious, he may have one or two toileting accidents in the new house. Don't get angry with him or you will make things worse. Simply clean up with an odour eliminator (see page 33) and put the dog outside more frequently, praising him when he goes in the correct place.

Take your dog on walks around his new neighbourhood and introduce him to neighbours.

Happy dog tip

Continue to feed and exercise your dog at his usual times, so that his routine is disrupted as little as possible. Act as normally as you can around him, as being over-attentive can actually create problems such as anxiety.

Happy travelling

It's lovely to be able to include your dog in your everyday life, and there is nothing more pleasant than a family outing to the park or beach. For many people this involves a trip in the car, so it is important that your dog feels quite happy and relaxed about travelling.

Some dogs associate the car with bad things, such as a trip to the vet or the boarding kennels, so creating more pleasant associations is one of the best ways to help him become a happy traveller. Keep your car well ventilated when your dog is travelling with you. Never leave him unattended in the car, as he can quickly become overheated which is potentially fatal.

Spray the fear away

Dogs show adverse reactions to the car for a number of reasons, ranging from travel sickness to fear or excitement. A short-term solution is to ask your vet to supply you with a dog-appeasing pheromone (DAP) spray (see page 34), which you can use to scent the inside of your car before setting off on your journey.

Using a travel crate

Some dogs love travelling in the car so much that they will bark and bounce around throughout the journey. This type of over-excitement can be very distracting for the driver and annoying for other passengers.

One way to help control this is to use a travel crate or pet carrier with a cover on it, as being able to see and move around in the car reinforces the dog's excitability. If your dog is not used to this, begin by feeding him in the crate and rewarding him with treats each time he goes inside. You can place his blanket or bed inside the crate to make him feel at home.

Most dogs that travel in a covered crate usually calm down quite quickly, and you can then gradually remove the cover for short distances but replace it if he starts barking again.

Medication

Although most motion sickness is caused by excitement rather than an adverse reaction to travel, it is nevertheless quite an unpleasant experience for both you and the dog. If you are going on a long journey that cannot be avoided, don't feed your dog for 12 hours before the

journey (but make sure he has access to fresh water), and if necessary seek veterinary advice about getting him a prescription for some anti-emetic medication, which will counteract the effects of travel sickness.

Happy travelling tips

- Don't forget to allow your dog time to toilet before he starts his journey.
- He should always travel behind a dog guard, preferably in a crate or on the back seat wearing a special dog harness.
- Be prepared: pack a small plastic bucket with a lid, a supply of cloths, some pet-safe disinfectant and a large bottle of water, so that you are ready to deal with any travel sickness or toileting accidents.
- Take food, water and bowls with you in the car. You can buy collapsible bowls, which are ideal for travelling.
- Put a chewy treat or toy in the dog's crate to keep him occupied while travelling.

Happy holidays

If your dog has become an integral member of the family and you can't bear to be parted from him, it's only natural that you will want him to enjoy a vacation with you. Luckily, recent changes to international legislation concerning animal quarantine have made it much easier for owners to travel abroad with their pets.

If you are planning to travel overseas, start organizing early as it takes several months to prepare the paperwork and get the necessary tests carried out.

All abroad!

Every country you plan to visit with your dog will have slightly different import requirements, so check with the authorities (for example, the embassy) of that country before you travel. Some countries have chosen to ban certain breeds of dog or require that they be muzzled in public places, so it is important to check that your dog is not on a list of banned breeds.

Many countries outside the European Union require an Export Health Certificate and/or an

import licence as well as other documents. Some countries require your dog to be injected against rabies within a specified period before his arrival (currently 30 days in the USA), so you may have to get him vaccinated before his booster is due.

Passports please

Some European countries may allow you to leave the country of origin but not re-enter without the correct paperwork. Dogs travelling with their owners in Europe will need a pet passport. To get a passport, your dog will need:

- Microchipping (see page 21).
- Rabies vaccination. Usually one injection will give immunity.
- Blood test. This must be taken 3–4 weeks after his rabies vaccine, to check that he's developed antibodies. If he doesn't pass this test, he can't travel. Occasionally a dog will fail the blood test, and must be re-vaccinated and blood tested to show antibodies.

Once your dog has a successful blood test result, he'll be issued with a passport. However, be aware that he may not be allowed to travel immediately – for example, in the UK dogs can only travel six months *after* a successful blood test.

Other requirements

Treatment for ticks and tapeworms Most European countries, including the UK, require that your dog is treated for these by an approved vet 24–48 hours before you return home.

Approved journey You must travel through a recognized route or port, so check your route first. At the port or airport, your dog will be scanned to check that his microchip matches his passport.

Disease When travelling abroad with your dog, he may be exposed to diseases he has not encountered before. Your vet can advise on how best to avoid these.

Stay-at-home vacations

The tourism industry now recognizes that many people like to holiday in their home country with their dog, and dog-friendly accommodation is widely available. The best places quickly become

fully booked, particularly during the high season, so book early to avoid disappointment.

A portable crate is the best way for your dog to travel whilst on holiday with you. He can sleep in it, and safely stay inside if you visit friends or a restaurant. You can also store his toys, blankets and bed inside.

Day trippers

A day at the beach, complete with a picnic, is a great excursion for everyone. Not all beaches are dog-friendly and there may be certain times of the year when dogs are off limits, so check first that you will be welcome. Tourism offices and holiday guides can advise.

For a day's outing to the beach, here are some of the things you will need to pack:

- Poop scoop or bags.
- Fresh drinking water.
- Bowls.
- Parasol, small tent or similar, for shade.
- Treats.
- Pet sunblock (if your dog has a pink nose).
- Towels.

If your dog enjoys swimming, don't allow him to stay in the water too long or swim out too far in case he gets into difficulties. Swimming is very tiring, and high tides can sweep a dog out to sea.

Happy boarding

There may be times when you feel you have no choice but to put your dog in a boarding kennel. Although you may worry that he will be unhappy while he's there, if you take the time to find a well established, clean, tidy and reputable facility the chances are he'll have a great time – although there's no doubt that he will be delighted to see you again at the end of his stay!

There are no guarantees that any kennel will be up to standard, so make some enquiries before you commit to a reservation. Begin with:

- Personal recommendation: ask your dog-owning friends where they send their dogs.
- Notice boards at your veterinary surgery, pet shop or grooming parlour.
- Local press.
- Telephone directories.
- Library.
- Internet.

Check points

Once you've drawn up a shortlist of kennels, arrange to visit them all. Cross any off your list that do not welcome your visits and/or will not allow you access to the entire facility.

First impressions Is it clean and tidy? Are there gaps between kennels to prevent the transmission of disease?

Licence Most local authorities will issue a certificate and this should be on display.

Vaccinations Avoid any kennel that will take pets without seeing up-to-date certificates.

Kennels Are they draught free? Is there heating at night? Do they look clean?

Daytime options

If you don't want to board your dog at a kennels during your working day, you could:
- Ask a neighbour to look after your dog.
- Employ a pet-sitter to visit during the day.
- Employ a house-sitter to look after your dog.

Exercise Are the dogs taken out for walks, alone or in a group? Do they have access to a run? If so, how often?

Cost Ask for the day rate. Does heating, special food or administering medications cost extra?

Illness What is the kennel's policy if your dog is taken ill while you are away?

Insurance What cover does the kennel owner have if your dog gets lost, injured or, worst of all, dies while in their care?

Canine hotels

There are some doggy hotels that offer such home comforts as armchairs, music, central heating, home-cooked cuisine and even supervised access to a heated doggy swimming pool. While these establishments cost more, you may decide that knowing your pet is living in the lap of luxury while you are away warrants the extra cost.

Day care

It is recommended that dogs are not left alone for longer than four hours or they can develop behavioural and psychological problems. Some kennels take dogs as day boarders, which is ideal for owners who work long hours and can't get home during the day. Simply drop off your dog in the morning and pick him up again after work, knowing he's had regular food and exercise.

Moving in

Whatever the facilities at the kennels you choose, to help him settle in more quickly, it is a good idea to pack your dog's favourite blankets, bed, toys and treats to take with him for his stay.

Good grief

Happy dogs enjoy close relationships with their owners, carers and other pets in the house. If and when a human or animal member of the family dies or even goes away for any length of time, everyone experiences a 'grief' reaction, including the family dog. So, how can you help your pet to cope when you are probably grieving yourself?

Of course, you may have the advantage of knowing that a situation is not permanent. Perhaps the dog's main carer has gone into hospital or away to college but is due back home in a few weeks, or your dog's canine pal is undergoing surgery and with luck will soon be returned safe and sound. Your dog, however, is unaware of this and may mope around searching for his friend, refusing to eat and play. It can be very upsetting.

RESEARCH
More scientific research is needed into the emotional lives of animals, but there is some evidence that wolves experience grief reactions. Wolves that have lost a pack member appear to mourn for several days, refusing to eat and spending their time lying down and moping.

Signs of grief
- Refusal to eat.
- Pacing and searching.
- Refusal to sleep.
- Sleeping too much.
- Lack of enthusiasm for play.
- Refusal to interact with other people or pets.
- Whining.
- Attention-seeking behaviour.

Act normally
Difficult as it may seem, the best way to help your dog return to his usual happy self is to act normally. Keep to his regular routine as much as possible and don't over-compensate for his loss by being more attentive than usual. This will simply

'Dogs can mirror their owner's emotions'

reinforce and reward his depressed behaviour patterns, and also risks complicating the situation by causing him to develop separation anxiety from you.

How to help

- Stick to your dog's regular timetable, but try taking him for longer walks and making an extra effort to distract him with new toys, treats and fun play sessions.
- Continue to offer food, but if he doesn't want to eat don't be tempted to offer new flavours and varieties. Simply take away uneaten food and encourage him to eat at the next meal, praising him when he does.
- Accept that your dog is going through a grieving process and let him recover in his own way. It can take several weeks before your happy dog re-emerges, but be reassured that eventually this will happen.
- If possible, act calmly. Dogs are extremely sensitive and their grief reactions may mirror the emotions they sense in their owner. If you

are constantly crying and sad, your dog will pick up on this and be very unhappy as well.
- Intervene as little as possible while remaining pets work out their own new pack positions. There may be a few squabbles and arguments among them until this is resolved.

New friend?

Don't be tempted to get another dog or family pet just to help your dog feel better. Do this only when you have recovered from the experience yourself, as otherwise you won't have the emotional and physical energy that a new pet deserves.

Happy dog tip

If you are concerned that your dog is very unhappy or depressed following the loss of a canine friend, do seek veterinary advice.

9 Taking on challenges

There are occasions when extraordinary situations crop up with your dog, which you can either embrace and enjoy or find overwhelming. Often, how we deal with life's challenges depends on the amount of control we have over the situation.

Sometimes we are ready for and welcome changes, perhaps making a decision to take on a retired working dog or a rescue dog. At other times we are presented with situations we don't feel ready or prepared for, such as when a dog suddenly develops special needs or disabilities. This chapter provides detailed advice on coping with both planned and unexpected changes.

Vanishing acts

One of the most distressing challenges an owner can face is if their dog goes missing. The reasons for this can include: being stolen, escaping, curiosity (a dog may decide to explore a workman's truck, then falls asleep and is driven away), frustration (unneutered dogs will stray to find a mate), trying to find a previous home or owner, disorientation and getting lost, falling or becoming trapped somewhere from which he can't escape.

What to do

- Prevention is always best, so get your dog microchipped and neutered (see pages 21 and 60–61).
- Put a tag on his collar indicating that he is microchipped.
- Check your garden regularly to ensure it is dog-proof.
- Keep recent photographs to use on fliers if your dog goes missing.
- Enlist family and friends to help search different areas.
- Repeat the searches at different times of day.
- Alert dog wardens, police, veterinary surgeries and animal shelters that your dog is missing.
- Place advertisements in local newspapers. Consider offering a reward.
- Create fliers and circulate as many as possible, posting them through neighbour's doors and pinning them on trees and lamp posts.
- Ask people to check sheds and garages where your dog may be trapped.
- Send a press release to local radio stations.
- Check the internet for sites that help to reunite owners with lost dogs.

Taking on a rescue dog

Adopting a rescue dog can seem a very kind and worthwhile gesture, but care must be taken to get the right dog for your family – love alone is never enough. With so many stray dogs picked up each year, there are thousands to choose from of all ages, colours and breed types.

RESEARCH
Studies show that 40 per cent of dogs enter rescue centres because of their owner's circumstances rather than any fault of their own. Reasons include death of an owner, redundancy, loss of home, moving abroad, divorce, mental health problems and so on. The other 60 per cent have some type of behaviour problems that their owners were unable to cope with. Thankfully most dogs with behaviour problems can be retrained and rehomed quite easily. A small minority have serious problems and can, therefore, only be rehomed to experienced owners.

Rescue dogs have already experienced many stressful situations, and although you may think that all they need is love to make them into happy, well-adjusted dogs, love alone is never enough. Talk to staff at the shelter to discuss what you can offer in terms of home, environment, time and family, and ask them to guide you to dogs that would be a good match.

Are you sure?

Before you seriously consider adopting a rescue dog, have an honest discussion with everyone in the family to ensure that they are all happy and excited about the idea. If one family member is not totally committed, don't go ahead.

How experienced are you? If your experience of dogs is limited or you have never owned one before, a rescue dog with an uncertain history may not be the best choice. Wait until you can confidently train, handle and cope with many different types of dog.

Be prepared to divulge some fairly personal information to rescue centres. Many will ask potential owners to fill in an extensive owner questionnaire and accept home visits to help assess their suitability.

Finding your rescue dog

The more information you have, the easier it is to decide whether you can give a particular dog a happy life. If the only details available are where he was picked up, whether he was neutered and the condition he was in, you will have to ask the staff for their honest assessment of his behaviour and personality type.

Dogs behave differently when they are living in kennels, but you can make a few assessments:

- If the dog comes to the front of his run when called, he is probably well socialized and confident so will suit a family home. If he prefers to stay warily at the back, he may be too timid for this and prefer a home where there are no children.
- Ask to see him being taken for a walk and then observe his reaction to kennel staff. If he struggles when they put on the lead, he may not be used to it and will need retraining. If he accepts the lead quietly and walks calmly, you can assume he has had some training and will be less problematic.
- Does he pull or seem reluctant to walk? Dogs that pull can be exhausting, so retraining and an experienced home may be required.
- How does he react to other dogs? Dogs that are aggressive with other dogs can be successfully rehomed, but care must be taken to find an experienced and confident owner who knows what they are taking on.
- Does he sit when asked? If so, this demonstrates he has had a basic level of training and means the rehoming process will be easier.
- Does he enjoy being petted? If so, he is obviously used to human contact and could thrive in a family home. If not, he may need resocializing and will suit a quieter home where there are no children.

Happy dog tip

If you can fall in love with your dog's character, rather than how he looks, it is a sure sign that your relationship will get off to a fantastic start.

Home time

Leaving the shelter and travelling in a strange car can be very stressful for a dog. Try to make the journey as calm as possible, putting the dog in a travel crate or dog harness so that he is not thrown around during the journey. Spraying the car or crate with DAP (see page 34) and playing some gentle classical music on the radio may help to appease his anxiety.

Make sure you have prepared everything beforehand and shopped for all the items you will need, so that you can relax and enjoy your time together. As soon as you arrive home, keep the dog on a lead and take him to the area of the garden where you want him to toilet. Allow him to walk around and explore the garden for a few minutes before you go indoors.

When you go inside, let him off the lead and give him plenty of time to investigate his new home, praising him as much as possible but gently correcting him if he does something you don't want, such as jumping up onto the sofa. Don't be afraid to establish house rules from the start.

Settling in

A rescue dog's first few days in his new home will be a little stressful for him but there are plenty of things you can do to make him feel more relaxed, confident and happy. Be patient but also consistent with any house rules you want him to adhere to, as one family member allowing a particular behaviour and another discouraging it can be very confusing for an already anxious dog.

You will probably find that you suddenly become very popular with friends and neighbours, who all want to come and say hello to your new dog. Although your dog should be encouraged to meet and socialize with all kinds of different people, limit this in the first day or two so that he doesn't become overwhelmed by all the attention.

Happy dog tip
Feed your dog the same food he ate at the kennels for the first few weeks. This will reduce the risk of him developing gastric upsets.

First night

When it gets to bedtime, take your dog outside to toilet and then try to settle him in his bed. Where he sleeps is really down to individual choice, but consider his background and personality type when you make this decision. If you know that in the past he has always been allowed to sleep close to his owner and he has a timid, sensitive nature, he may settle better if his bed is placed either in your bedroom or just outside the door. Boisterous, dominant dogs will probably be better left in the kitchen overnight, even if they don't agree with your decision!

Be firm, and don't keep going back to reassure your dog or shout at him if he barks, scratches and howls. If you think he needs to toilet, don't speak to him at all but simply take him outside on a lead and wait until he goes, then put him back on his bed. In time he will settle down and you can enjoy a peaceful night's sleep once more.

If you think your dog is likely to scratch at the door on his first night, protect the woodwork with a temporary cover of carpet or a sheet of Perspex.

Routine

Establish a regular routine for your dog's feeding, walking and sleeping arrangements as soon as you can. This will help him to adjust to his new surroundings and make him feel secure. Although you may want to spend every minute with him, train him to spend increasing amounts of time calmly and quietly on his own, so that he doesn't become over-dependent and experience anxiety when you are not in the room. Start by leaving him for five minutes and gradually build up to longer periods.

Good manners

From the beginning, insist that your dog behaves with good manners around other people and pets. If necessary, keep him on a lead when you have visitors, and give them some titbits or treats to feed him so that he begins to associate them with positive experiences.

Encourage children to understand that their new pet is not a toy, and for the first few days ask them to allow the dog to come to them rather than the other way round. It can be difficult, especially with very young children, so supervise them continually and don't leave them in a room with the dog when you are not present.

House training

Some dogs that have been in a rescue shelter for a long time may need retraining to toilet outdoors. Take your dog outside as much as possible and give him lots of walks. Praise him enthusiastically when he toilets in the right place. If he does have an accident, take him outside to where he should have gone and clean up the area thoroughly to discourage him from going back there again.

Taking on a retired working dog

If you think you can give a home to a rejected or retired working dog, you could just end up with a fabulous family friend. For example, some hearing or guide dogs fail to pass the rigorous tests required to do their job safely, perhaps because they startle easily or are a little apprehensive, but that doesn't mean they won't settle very happily into family life.

Military and police services often retire their dogs and then seek good homes for them, but be prepared to undergo some rigorous testing before you are accepted as a suitable owner.

Roles dogs play

The range of working dogs includes:
- Assistance dogs for physically disabled handlers, including guide dogs for the blind and hearing dogs for the deaf.
- Therapy dogs (see pages 110–111).
- Hunting and tracker dogs.
- Cadaver dogs, which locate fatalities at scenes of crime or disaster.
- Mountain and water rescue dogs.
- Detection dogs, which help to locate many things such as drugs at airports, termite colonies in houses, cancerous growths (by smelling breath, trained dogs can detect lung cancer and breast cancer in the very early stages – sometimes much earlier than a CAT or MRI scanner), or warn handlers about the onset of an epileptic fit.
- Police dogs, which assist with crowd control and apprehending criminals.
- Herding dogs, which help to control and move livestock.
- Guard and watch dogs.
- Sled dogs.

Working dogs as pets

The breeding of working dogs has resulted in them being extremely intelligent, hardy and alert. They are often attractive in appearance and can be extremely loyal. Because of this, many working breeds are sought after as family pets, but owners who fail to understand fully the level of companionship, exercise and stimulation these dogs require are unlikely to be able to cope with their demands.

Working dogs can make excellent pets, but to keep them happy potential owners must realize that they need to be given 'work' to do. Dogs that are not going to be used for their original purpose must be trained from a young age, as they will still retain all their natural hunting, herding or scenting instincts. Activities such as obedience training, flyball, dancing and agility, informal or novelty shows and trial work are all excellent channels for these energetic breeds. In addition, they will also need plenty of walking and other exercise in the form of games and playing, plus lots of interaction with their human carers. These dogs are therefore best suited to physically active individuals and families.

Retired service dogs

Service dogs such as hearing or guide dogs (often referred to as 'seeing eye' dogs), are not expected to work indefinitely, as in time their health and abilities will inevitably diminish. Most retire between the ages of eight and ten years, and if their disabled owner or a family member is unable to keep them they will be offered for adoption.

Although the bond between yourself and such a dog is unlikely to become as strong as the one he experienced with his disabled owner, these are nevertheless very intelligent, well-trained dogs (some knowing up to 40 different verbal commands) and make wonderful family pets. There is often quite a long waiting list for adopting a retired service dog, so contact the organization that trains puppies and put your name on the list.

Ex-racers

Retired Greyhounds can also make wonderful family pets once their racing career is over, which is usually between the ages of four and six years. They are very gentle and adaptable dogs, but it is important to remember that such a dog will not have lived in a house or experienced a lot of love and attention, so will need patience and some retraining. However, it is incredibly rewarding to watch a Greyhound blossom into a happy, loving family pet.

Contrary to popular opinion, Greyhounds do not need a lot of exercise: a couple of 20-minute walks each day is ideal. Because your dog will have been trained to chase a mechanical lure, it is advisable to keep him on a lead as his instinct to chase can

Happy dog tip

Don't allow a working dog to become bored or understimulated, as he may develop behaviour patterns to try to reduce his stress levels. Some can be problematic and include constant barking, scratching at doors, or trying to escape and find entertainment elsewhere!

lead him into dangerous situations such as oncoming traffic – and although he is probably no more likely to chase cats than other breeds, he is more likely to catch them! Contact a Greyhound welfare organization for further information on adopting these lovely dogs.

Providing a safe haven

Many working dogs, such as Border Collies, are very sensitive and appreciate having a quiet place in which they can take refuge when they are not working. Some herding dogs have very sensitive hearing and will appreciate a hidey-hole if there is a thunderstorm, you are vacuuming or there are lots of noisy children around.

Coping with a disabled dog

If your dog develops special needs, perhaps through illness or accident, it can be very upsetting. However, the good news is that dogs adapt and cope quite happily with disability. They have an amazing ability to adjust to situations and can certainly teach us a lot about the value of not being self-conscious but simply getting on with enjoying life.

As far as coping goes, dogs have many advantages, including an incredible sense of smell that enables them to navigate and recognize their whereabouts. With a little planning and some home adjustments, you can make life very happy for your disabled dog.

Coping with blindness

Dogs often lose their sight in old age, and usually this is a gradual deterioration attributed to the ageing process. Some dogs are born blind and people are often astounded to discover that this is the case, as they cope so well and give no outward signs of disability. Other dogs lose the sight of one or both eyes through illness or injury and adjust very quickly to their condition. Nevertheless,

RESEARCH
Studies show that dogs can hear sounds up to 67 kHz compared with up to 20 kHz for humans. However, the sensitivity *range* is similar, which means that dogs' hearing can be tested using similar techniques to those used for humans.

there are several ways in which you can help:

- Keep furniture in the same place, so the dog can learn to navigate around it.
- Consider applying aromatherapy scents to areas you don't want the dog to go. Gravel or sand can act as a marker for prohibited garden areas.
- Place food and water bowls in a familiar place.
- Try not to intervene as your dog adjusts to being blind. Instead, encourage him to be independent.

Coping with deafness

As with humans, old age can result in hearing loss for dogs. However, some breeds are more prone to deafness than others: for example, an estimated 22 per cent of Dalmatians are affected in the UK and as many as 30 per cent in the USA.

However, it's important to remember that a deaf dog has only lost one of his senses. The key to good communication is through exaggerated visual signals, such as a wave or holding your hand out in front of you. Toys and treats can help to keep the dog focused and should be used as rewards every time he responds to hand signals.

You can buy collars that vibrate gently to get your dog's attention, and also beep to help you find him (alternatively, you can put a bell on his collar). However, these collars only work within a limited range of approximately 100 m (110 yd), so hand signals are still important.

Some owners use a small hand-held light, such as a keyring with an LED, to help train their dog. He will learn to react to the light snapping on and off quickly in the same way as a hearing dog reacts to a clicker (see page 75).

All in all, there is no reason why, with patience and plenty of time, a deaf dog should be any less trainable than one with full hearing.

Mobility problems

Dogs usually cope very well with the loss (surgical amputation) of a limb, whether due to injury or disease. Loss of a front limb is more difficult, as dogs bear most of their weight on the front legs. However, within days of surgery and once the wound has healed most dogs are able to adjust to walking on three legs. Weeks later they are usually able run and play as easily as their four-legged friends, and many owners report that people they meet are astonished to be told that a dog has a leg missing as they hadn't noticed any mobility impairment.

There is usually no need to limit the amount of exercise, and the more mobile your dog is the better. Your vet will probably refer him to a qualified animal physiotherapist, who will work with your dog during his convalescence and recommend exercises to help him recover and regain his strength and mobility. Regular canine hydrotherapy sessions, where the dog is put in a harness and swims in a heated pool, can also help as this is a non-weightbearing exercise that encourages better muscle tone. Acupuncture can also be very useful to help reduce pain, increase mobility and give a better quality of life.

Dogs that have lost the use of one or more limbs but are pain free and still appear to enjoy life may benefit from a specially developed canine paraplegic cart. This can give a dog some independence and he will be more comfortable than dragging himself along the ground.

10 Happiness in old age

In recent years there have been so many developments in veterinary medicine, nutrition and the understanding of behaviour that dogs are now living longer than ever. Their average lifespan has increased from seven years in the 1930s to more than 12 years. Most dogs are considered senior by the time they reach their eighth birthday but many go on to live much longer, and smaller breeds can live to 20 years and beyond.

Old age is not an illness, and if you remain alert to potential problems there is no reason why your older dog should not be very happy during the later years of his life. This chapter explains how to look after your dog as he ages, starting with the check points below:

Nutrition The digestive system gradually becomes less effective in old age, so good nutrition is vital.

Dental care Regular cleaning, combined with a sensible diet can help prevent problems with teeth and gums.

Exercise 'Little and often' is the key to keeping joints supple.

Grooming Older dogs may need extra help to keep clean. Regular grooming also provides the opportunity to check for bumps, lumps and cuts.

Vaccinations and worming Worming should continue throughout your dog's life. There is debate over the continuing necessity for vaccinations in an older dog (see page 153).

Geriatric clinic

Enquire at your veterinary surgery to see if they have a geriatric clinic. These are often run by the practice nurse and the service may even be free. It is a wonderful opportunity for your dog to be weighed and examined. His blood pressure and urine will be checked, and his teeth, eyes and ears examined. You will also get lots of expert advice on feeding and behaviour problems.

Life for the older dog

Although providing a good diet, regular exercise and a stress-free environment will help to keep your dog happy and improve the quality of his life, it is still quite difficult to predict how long he will live. Dogs are said to age 12 times faster than humans, which means an 18-month-old dog is the equivalent of an 18-year-old person – although thankfully the ageing process slows down after the first couple of years!

When it comes to longevity, much will depend on your dog's breed, size and medical history. In general, small breeds tend to live longer than large ones – the average age for small breeds is 15 years, for larger dogs ten years (although sometimes less for giant breeds).

Physical changes

Some age-related changes are more noticeable than others, which is why it is important to have your older dog checked regularly by your vet. Common changes include:

Musculosketal Muscle mass decreases and painful joint problems such as arthritis can develop, affecting his mobility and behaviour.

Vision Many older dogs develop cataracts. You may notice your dog's eyes becoming cloudy and that he has difficulty seeing.

Hearing Some dogs can feel vibration so if yours loses hearing try stamping your foot as you call his name. He will be vulnerable to road accidents, so in urban areas keep him on a lead.

RESEARCH
Trials with drugs for Parkinson's disease in humans have been shown to be useful in some dogs with behaviour problems caused by age-related cognitive changes such as circling, tremors, compulsive behaviours and inappropriate vocalization.

Toileting Dogs that develop kidney problems may urinate more. Some start soiling in the house, which is frustrating for owners.

Obesity As your dog becomes less mobile he may put on weight. It's important to control obesity, to prevent this affecting his mobility further and putting a strain on vital organs.

Going grey

As with us, the pigment of a dog's hair will change over the years and older dogs can develop white or grey hairs. These tend to appear first by the whiskers and then spread over the nose and head.

Slowing down

Many owners with senior dogs notice that they gradually slow down. Perhaps the dog seems to be taking longer to make his way up and down the stairs, is reluctant to jump off the bed, or is walking slowly and running less.

If you begin to notice this, don't just assume that it is due to the ageing process. You should seek veterinary attention, as there may well be an underlying health problem that can be treated easily. With suitable medication, your dog could soon return to a second flush of youth!

Behaviour

Some older dogs become more congenial in old age, others turn into real grumps! If your dog undergoes a total personality change, don't just assume it's down to getting old – ask your vet to rule out illness or pain as contributory factors.

Your dog may eat and drink less or more. Check his gums and teeth and ask your vet to rule out a metabolic cause.

He may also sleep more, but try to ensure he exercises regularly to help with mobility. Dogs with mobility problems cannot easily escape from stressful situations and may nip or growl, so supervise older dogs and children at all times.

If your older dog was 'pack leader' in a multi-dog house, the younger dogs may challenge him for this position. There may be a few squabbles until this is resolved. It's probably best to intervene as little as possible, unless fighting is severe and there is a big difference in the size of the dogs so that the risk of injury is increased. If the situation does not improve, seek the advice of a professional behaviour counsellor. Some older dogs that have been 'demoted' may take a while to adjust to their new position.

If your dog can no longer follow you from room to room he may feel isolated and depressed. See pages 148–149 for tips on how to deal with this.

Care for the elderly

Sadly, older dogs in rescue centres are often overlooked in favour of puppies. Many shelters have foster schemes to try to find temporary homes for older dogs until an owner is found. Dogs are so much happier in a home environment than in a shelter, and usually settle very quickly. If you are interested in becoming a foster carer, contact your local rescue centre to offer your services.

Adapting your home and routine

There are many things you can do to make sure your dog's later years are as enjoyable as possible. Even very small changes can make an enormous difference to his quality of life. If you have lived with your dog for several years, you are the best authority to gauge his emotional and physical requirements.

Compare your dog's behaviour now to the previous year and assess the changes. There will be some things he is no longer able to do, but with effort and imagination you should be able to come up with some innovative solutions.

Beds and cushions

If your senior dog has mobility problems and finds it difficult to follow you around the house as he used to, it can make him feel very isolated and depressed. Moving his daytime bed to a central area of the room in which he rests can help to overcome this, by making him more like part of the family again.

As your dog's muscle mass decreases, lying down on a hard surface becomes less comfortable. Placing extra cushions and beds next to radiators throughout the house is the perfect remedy.

Hot and cold

Older dogs often feel the cold more and yours will probably appreciate a coat for when you go out walking together. If he comes in wet from a walk, dry him off thoroughly and put an extra-cosy blanket in his bed to keep him warm.

Some older dogs will not realize they are overheating, so watch him carefully in hot weather. Don't allow him to sleep all day in full sunlight in a porch or conservatory, and if he is outside make sure he moves to a cooler area or indoors when the sun is at its hottest.

Thinning hair around the ears and nose may make older dogs more prone to sunburn. Protect your dog's skin by applying pet sunblock to these vulnerable areas.

Stepping up

Older dogs may have difficulty climbing up onto an armchair on which they previously enjoyed sleeping. Placing a low wooden box or steps next to it will help him to get up and down, and if you do the same near a window he can continue to stand up and enjoy watching the world go by, just as he always did.

Getting around

Musculoskeletal changes can make it difficult for an old dog to walk on hard, slippery surfaces such as vinyl, tiles or wood. You can help him get about by placing some non-skid rugs around the house.

Routine

An older dog will enjoy life much more if he has a set routine for feeding, exercise and toileting. Stick to this as much as you can and avoid moving furniture around too much, particularly if he has vision problems.

Caution

Don't punish or scold an older dog if he has an accident in the house, as he may not be able to help it. Kidney function does deteriorate in older dogs, so seek veterinary advice. Be patient and calm, and try to think of ways to avoid the problem, such as keeping him on a lead so that you know when he needs to toilet.

Your elderly dog will find it more difficult than a younger one to cope with changes such as a house move or an influx of visitors. It may be better to settle him safely in his crate during a visit from rowdy children or if building work is being carried out. However, don't forget that dogs are social creatures and he will not enjoy feeling isolated from family life for long periods.

Exercise and nutrition

These two closely-related areas can make a huge difference to how long your dog is able to enjoy living life to the full. He will begin to slow down, and you will have to adjust his exercise accordingly. You may also need to think about changing his diet to cater for his changing nutritional needs.

As your dog begins to slow down, you will need to remember that it is going to take him longer to do things such as standing up and lying down, going for walks, and climbing in and out of your car. Make sure you allow the extra time needed so that you do not become impatient, which may upset him, or try to rush him around, which may cause him physical discomfort.

Nutrition

An enormous range of wet and dry food developed especially for senior dogs is now available, both from your vet and over the counter at your pet store. However, just because your dog is a senior doesn't necessarily mean you have to change his diet. If he's happy and healthy and his weight is stable, then why make changes?

Eventually, however, his metabolism is likely to slow down, and if he's not exercising as much he will need to consume fewer calories to avoid piling on the pounds. Senior 'light' formulas have been developed using ingredients to make your dog feel full while consuming fewer calories. In addition, your older dog's liver and kidneys are likely to become less efficient and these can be supported with a suitable diet.

Your veterinary surgery is an excellent source of advice and information on feeding a senior dog, so don't hesitate to make an appointment and find out what foods are available and which is most suited to your dog's breed, size and weight.

Any treats that your dog eats must be included in the total calories he consumes, so try to reward your dog with verbal praise and physical contact or a game, rather than relying on food.

Older dogs may have more sensitive digestive systems and be vulnerable to bacterial infection, so keep food bowls scrupulously clean and refresh water supplies frequently to reduce the risk.

Supplements

A huge range of food supplements is available for you to buy for your senior dog, but check with your vet before doing so. Feeding supplements can interfere with the nutritional balance of some complete or prescription diets, so you could be wasting your money and actually doing your dog more harm than good. Common supplements are:

Glucosamine and chondroitin Can reduce the painful symptoms of degenerative joint disease. Glucosamine is a natural sugar produced by the body, which helps to stimulate the production of molecules that produce healthy joint cartilage. Chondroitin (from shark cartilage) works with glucosamine to help repair damaged cartilage.

Vitamin A Helps with bone formation and the growth and repair of body tissues.

Vitamin B12 Believed to help increase energy levels and boost metabolism.

Vitamin C Boosts the immune system.

Vitamin E An antioxidant which helps to protect against free radicals (unstable molecules that can cause oxidation and damage to cells). Airborne emissions, sunlight, chemical sources and pollution can all create free radicals and speed up ageing, increasing risk of disease.

Omega 3 and 6 fatty acids Constituents of fish oils. Said to have anti-inflammatory properties.

Yucca Long associated with the treatment of rheumatism and arthritis. The root is rich in sponins, substances that are said to help the body produce natural cortisone.

Frequent feeds

Consider feeding your older dog three or four smaller meals each day rather than two large ones. This will prevent him becoming hungry between feeds and encourage him to burn calories more efficiently throughout the day. Introduce any changes very gradually.

Exercise

When it comes to exercising older dogs, less is definitely more. Even if your dog no longer asks to go out for a walk, it is important to take him two or three times a day. The more gentle exercise he gets, the better it will be for his joints.

- Exercise your dog before feeding and wait half an hour before you provide a meal.
- Walk slowly for five minutes to warm up his muscles, more briskly for 15 to 20 minutes, and then slow the pace again for the final five minutes to allow him to cool down. Avoid jogging with your older dog.
- If he enjoys fetching a ball, continue to do this but for less time and over shorter distances.
- If your dog exhibits shortness of breath or extreme fatigue after walking, consult your vet.

Health tips

Even if your dog has been lucky enough to enjoy good health throughout his puppy and young adult years, he will become more vulnerable to disease as he ages. This is simply due to natural deterioration of his organs, bones, skin and metabolism.

For example, some dogs can become much more sensitive to sound, and although previously unfazed by thunderstorms will suddenly develop phobic behaviour. Conversely, dogs that lose their hearing can sometimes no longer hear scary sounds such as fireworks and will remain blissfully unaware of what is going on. However, there are some preventative health measures you can take to help retard and/or alleviate some of the effects of the ageing process.

Fleas and ticks

Changes to a dog's skin and immune system in old age can make him more vulnerable to flea- and tick-bite allergies. Embark on a rigorous control programme and stick to it. Flea treatments will also help to control ticks.

- Begin by using a brush and flea comb on your dog several times a week to comb out any eggs and living fleas.
- Ask your vet for advice on the most gentle but effective product that will help to kill fleas and disrupt their reproductive cycle. The simplest involve just dropping the contents of a capsule onto the dog's neck once a month.
- Treat your home and car regularly for flea infestation using an anti-flea preparation available from your vet or pet store.
- Avoid 'layering' treatments, such as washing in flea shampoos, using a collar and applying flea control medication. This could overload your older dog's system and may cause side effects.

Happy dog tip

Avoid putting a flea collar that comes ready-drenched with insecticides on your ageing dog, as he may be more prone to side effects. Instead, if you have such a collar drop it into your vacuum bag to kill off any fleas that you vacuum up.

'Check with your vet before giving your dog any human medications, as some can be very dangerous for your pet'

Vaccinations

Ask your vet to explain the surgery's policy on vaccinating older dogs. Some vets argue for vaccination, because they reason that an older dog's immune system is less effective and if he contracts a disease it will be more difficult to fight off. Others consider it unnecessary to vaccinate a dog over the age of ten years, because they feel the immune system can be compromised and by the time they reach that age dogs have a sufficient level of protection. It is ultimately your choice whether or not to proceed.

In any case, recent developments in veterinary science and vaccines mean that apart from an annual rabies jab (which is a requirement in parts of the USA and if you are travelling with your dog), your dog may now require booster vaccines only once every three years.

Complementary therapies

Many complementary therapies are available, some of which claim to cure a wide range of dog ailments. However, apart from acupuncture, there is little scientific data to support this. Some vets offer therapies such as homeopathy or herbalism, but in any case you should always seek veterinary advice before embarking on complementary treatments for your pet.

Bach flower remedies These are available over the counter and contain minute doses of plant extract which help combat various emotional and physical problems. Some owners report that Bach Rescue Remedy, which contains several plant extracts, is useful in calming stressed dogs.

Aromatherapy This non-invasive therapy uses powerful essential oils extracted from plants such as lavender, rose and geranium. The oils are inhaled or absorbed by the dog by licking, and practitioners claim they can benefit pets with emotional, physical and behaviour problems.

Know your dog's 'normals'

If your dog is healthy, his vital signs will fall within the following parameters:
Temperature 37.5–39.3°C (99.5–102.8°F)
Pulse 60–120 beats per minute
Breathing 14–22 breaths per minute
If your dog shows signs of illness and his pulse, breathing and/or temperature fall outside these ranges, consult your vet for further advice.

Tellington Touch A gentle technique developed in the USA by Linda Tellington-Jones. It involves special 'Ttouches', leg lifts and other moves, designed to release tension and increase body awareness. Once a therapist has shown you how to do the moves, you can practise these with your dog at home.

Shiatsu The Japanese word for 'finger pressure', this is a sister treatment to acupuncture. Practitioners use their hands instead of needles to apply pressure and stretches to the dog's body.

Happy endings

Sadly, none of us lives forever, but knowing this doesn't make it any easier to lose a dog that was a special friend. Thankfully, it is quite rare to lose a healthy dog without any warning or be forced into a rushed decision. Although it can be painful, taking a little time now to consider what you and your family would like to happen if your dog becomes too old or ill to enjoy life, can help ease the burden later on.

You have done so much to make sure that your dog has had a happy life, the last thing you can do for him is ensure that he has a happy and peaceful ending.

Euthanasia

Sometimes referred to as 'putting to sleep', euthanasia is what vets do when a pet is suffering too much or has very little quality of life. You will probably know when the time for this is near, but most owners delay the decision as long as possible, hoping that nature will take its course. Although your vet will be happy to talk things through and explain what is involved, the decision will ultimately be yours.

Try to involve everyone in the family in the decision, including children. This will probably their first experience of dealing with death and grief, so the more involved they are in the decision, the easier it will be for them to come to terms with it. Often, children are very resilient and pragmatic, and are able to accept the situation more quickly than adults in the family.

When is the right time?

There is no need to feel guilty about making the very difficult decision to have your dog put to sleep. After everything you have done to give him a happy life, your last act of kindness can be to help end his suffering and give him a peaceful death.

Sometimes the decision can be fairly straightforward – for example, if your dog has been badly injured in a road accident – but at other times the decision is more complicated and stems from your relationship with the dog, how you view his quality of life and what you consider to be the best option for him.

To help you decide, here are some things for you to think about, and if you are at all uncertain your vet will give you his honest, professional opinion. Consider euthanasia if your dog:

- Is in constant pain.
- Is blind and deaf and has difficulty coping.
- Cannot eat or drink.
- Cannot stand up or move.
- Has organ failure.
- Is incontinent.
- You cannot cope financially or emotionally with caring for him.

Happy dog tip

If your dog is highly strung, you can keep him calm and happy by arranging for him to be given a tranquillizer prior to the vet arriving or before visiting the surgery.

What will happen?

Before you make an appointment, consider what you want to happen to your dog's body.

- If you want to bury him in the garden, check with your local authority and before your appointment arrange to dig a hole that is at least 60 cm (2 ft) deep. You may not feel up to this after the event.
- If you prefer to have your dog cremated discuss this with your vet, particularly if you want the ashes returned.
- If your dog is to be buried in a pet cemetery, once you have made an appointment you will need to let the company know when they can pick him up.
- If you do not feel up to dealing with your dog's body, you can ask your vet to do so.

You can arrange for the vet to visit your house, or make an appointment to visit the surgery where all the necessary facilities are available.

Consider whether you feel strong enough to hold the dog during this final visit. Don't feel guilty if you can't: lots of people find it too much to bear and worry that breaking down in tears will distress the dog. However, if you can remain calm and hold him throughout you will undoubtedly be a comforting presence.

The vet will shave a small area of fur from the dog's front leg and then inject him with a fatal overdose of medicine (usually a barbiturate, pentobarbitone) that is similar to a powerful anaesthetic. Within seconds your dog will fall asleep, and very shortly afterwards his heart will stop beating and his breathing will cease. There may be a gasp as his body relaxes and occasionally this will cause him to empty his bowels or bladder.

Be assured that euthanasia is a fast and completely painless procedure. Your dog will simply drift off into a deep and peaceful sleep from which he will not wake.

Happy memories

Once your initial grief, sadness and sometimes anger at losing your dog has passed, you will gradually start to enjoy thinking about all the happy times you spent together. There are many ways to commemorate your dog's life and celebrate what a special friend he was to you.

By taking positive steps in this way, you will mark the end of your mourning and begin to move forward, just as your dog would want you to do.

Owners and grief

There is no doubt that you will feel horribly sad when your dog passes away, either from natural causes or through euthanasia. The length of time for which each person grieves will vary.

Research into grieving reveals that there are several distinct stages to the process. It is necessary to experience each stage before moving on to the next and eventual healing. The stages of grief are:

Anticipated loss Particularly with a prolonged illness or euthanasia. Owners begin to say goodbye to their dog and may begin to detach themselves emotionally to prepare for his death.

Shock and denial This is often experienced immediately after death, although it can be accompanied by an initial feeling of relief, particularly if the dog has been suffering for a long time.

Emotional pain and suffering These are the middle phases of a grief reaction and when you are likely to feel most tearful and upset.

Recovery Finally, owners begin to accept the situation and start to find meaning and comfort when recalling the life and death of their dog.

Don't rush the process – just accept that you are going to be sad, and arrange to be around people who will allow you to talk about your dog and cry for him without making you feel silly or guilty.

Unfortunately, some people can get emotionally 'locked' into one of the stages and this is when professional bereavement counselling can be very useful. Veterinary nurses are often trained in bereavement counselling, so take advantage of this if available. Some animal welfare charities also run telephone or e-mail support services.

When you are feeling better (which can take many months), you may feel able to help out as a befriender, sharing the wisdom of your experience with someone else who is grieving for their pet.

Dogs and grief

There is evidence that some dogs appear to grieve at the loss of a companion, perhaps by becoming withdrawn, losing their appetite and experiencing erratic sleep patterns. It is not clear whether the dog is reacting to his owner's distress, the loss of a friend or a combination of both, but whatever the case it is important not to overreact to any of his behavioural changes as this will reinforce and prolong the problem. Try not to pet the dog constantly or give him too much attention. You can help the dog by sticking to your regular routine as much as possible.

In time, things will return to normal. If the dog that was lost was a very dominant character, you may even find that the remaining dog appears to relish his new position in the house and becomes much more extrovert than he was before.

Memories

There are lots of ways in which you can remember your dog. Here are some you might like to consider that will help to make you smile again:

- Commission a painting from a favourite photograph of your dog.
- Make a collage of pictures.
- Ask your children to write a poem or make a scrapbook about the dog.
- Plant a rose in his favourite spot in the garden.
- Create a corner for some quiet reflection; this can be indoors or out, as long as it is a place you can go to enjoy thinking about your time together.
- Commission a plaque or an engraved casket for your dog's ashes.
- Get creative and write a song or funny story about some of the exploits and mischief he used to get up to.

Moving on

Eventually, when enough time has passed and you are feeling stronger, you may decide that your days are rather empty without a dog to love and have fun with. You may start to think that you're ready to fill another dog's life with happiness.

Although a new dog will never replace the friend you lost, he will bring you a different kind of joy and help you to build new happy memories. Think of it as a way of reinvesting the love that you gave to your former friend. Only you will know in your heart when the time is right, but it is generally when you are able to think about your dog and smile instead of crying.

Index

Acknowledgements

Over the years, so many clever and knowledgeable people have been generous with their time and helped me to learn how to care for the animals with which we share our lives. Without these people (too many to mention individually, but you know who you are), I would not have had the confidence and determination to write this book. Special thanks go to my lovely daughter, Madeline Joy, whose unconditional love sustains me always. Thanks also to her Daddy, William Mark Lainchbury, BSc, MRCVS, for all his technical support, veterinary advice and personal encouragement. And to Pepe, the little Yorkshire Terrier who has travelled through life with me for so long and given me a huge amount of fun and happiness. Thank you all very much.

Executive Editor Trevor Davies
Editors Alice Bowden, Lisa John
Executive Art Editor Darren Southern
Designer Maggie Town, One2Six Creative
Picture Library Manager Jennifer Veall
Senior Production Controller Martin Croshaw

Picture Acknowledgements
Alamy /Thorsten Eckert 155; /Jack Sullivan 143.
Ardea /John Daniels 127, 150; /Jean Michel Labat 31, 147.
Corbis UK Ltd 85, 123, 144; /George Disario 59; /Larry Hirshowitz 30; /Christian Liepe 134; /LWA-Dann Tardiff 115; /Markus Moellenberg 4; /Star Ledger/Christopher Barth 1 130; /Randy M. Urg 103; /Larry Williams 20; /Zefa/Markus Botzek 75.
DK Images /Tim Ridley 80, 81.
Getty Images 56; /Birgid Alliq 131; /Mojgan Azimi 112; /John W Banagan 139; /Adri Berger 97; /Christopher Bissell 1 ' ' /Blue Line Pictures 133; /Paul Bricknell 51 t ʳ Cade 76, 157; /Stewart Charles Cohen /Jim Cooper 16; /Jim Craigmyle 140; Robert Daly 86; /Peter Dazeley 22; Patricia Doyle 29, 60, 124; /Jerry Drury 83; /Safia Fatimi 142; / ʳn Francis 52; /John Giustina 100; 88, 92, 117; /Paul Harris 33; / nk Herholdt 102; /Sean Justice 101; /Ashley Karyl 118; /Kathi Lamm 10; /Tony Latham 151; /Bruce Laurance 58; /Lecorre Productions 125; / G & M David de Lossy 110, 138; /Steve Lyne 15; /Silvestre Machado 95; /Robert Manella 137; /Kaz Mori 94; /Jean Moss 89; /Sean Murphy 111; /Neo Vision 2, 8, 48, 57, 156; /Daly & Newton 129; /Diane Padys 120; /Barbara Peacock 128; /Petrography 79, 132; /Plant 98; /Gary Randall 13; /Lisa M Robinson 119; /Jo Sax 12, 42; /Steve Shott 77, 149; /Daq Sundberg 141; /Jeffrey Sylvester 14, 96; /Paul Viant 122; /David Ward 105.
Octopus Publishing Group Limited 19, 64, 65; /Stephen Conroy 90, 91; /Janeanne Gilchrist 108-109; /Steve Gorton 18, 24, 43, 50, 54, 55, 66, 68, 72, 93; /Rosie Hyde 23, 35, 69, 116; /Ray Moller 40, 41, 46 top right, 46 bottom left, 47 top right, 47 bottom left; /John Moss 152; /Angus Murray 11, 32, 44, 51, 71, 74, 104, 121, 126; /Tim Ridley 136, 154; /Russell Sadur 148, 153.
Photodisc 17, 28, 38, 39.
Victor Steel Photography 107.
Warren Photographic 1, 62, 63.